Eight Months Behind the Bamboo Curtain

In memory of my beloved father, Chang Chia-yee,
who taught me that justice will always triumph.

Eight Months Behind the Bamboo Curtain

A Report on the First Eight Months of Communist Rule in China

Chang Kuo-sin

CITY UNIVERSITY OF
HONG KONG PRESS
香港城市大學出版社

Disclaimer: Chang Kuo-sin's text is published as originally written, with no edits or amendments.

ISBN: 978-962-937-288-0

Published by
   City University of Hong Kong Press
   Tat Chee Avenue
   Kowloon, Hong Kong
   Website: www.cityu.edu.hk/upress
   E-mail: upress@cityu.edu.hk

Printed in Hong Kong

Table of Contents

PART TWO

Communist Rule in China After Eight Months of Trial (April – December 1949)

Foreword

Mr. Chang Kuo-sin's *Eight Months Behind the Bamboo Curtain* is a book of historical significance as it is a rare first-person account of China's transformation from capitalism to communism. As a correspondent of the United Press (now United Press International) in Nanking, Mr. Chang witnessed the fall of the city to communist forces in April 1949. While the communists barred him from transmitting information to the news agency, he took copious notes of how life in the city changed as the Chinese Communist Party imposed its reign. On arriving in Hong Kong in October 1949, he turned his notes into a series of articles – followed by a book in 1950 – which revealed to the world the truth about life under communist rule in China.

More than sixty years later, his observations on the pitfalls of communist rule have stood the test of time. He observed that "The Chinese communists would have to change their ways or they would ultimately fail" and that "as communists, they would succeed, while their communism would not". The tumultuous changes that China went through during the first thirty years of communist rule and the Chinese Communist Party's decision to develop "socialism with Chinese characteristics" over the past forty years have proved that Mr. Chang's observations were prescient.

The book also shows the depth and breadth of skills Mr. Chang possessed as a journalist, including being an adept listener, interviewer, observer and writer with an extensive knowledge of history and politics. These are skills that young journalists can hone by reading his vivid accounts of a momentous period in Chinese history. Through his accounts, readers are able to reconstruct in their minds how the well-disciplined People's Liberation Army took orderly control of Nanking and Shanghai and how the disorderly Nationalist army's retreat degenerated into chaos. Equally well reported was the transformation of people's initial euphoria towards the communists to that of resentment as totalitarian control sank in. Chang's reports on how the communists dealt with the foreign press and non-communist political parties shed light on what freedom of speech and thought – or the lack of it – would mean in communist China.

From 1978 to 1985, as head of the Department of Communication of the then Hong Kong Baptist College, Mr. Chang conceived and imparted to students the idea of "truth is virtue" and made it the motto of the department. Since then, the department has become the School of

Communication and the college the Hong Kong Baptist University. Despite the passage of time, the motto's power to inspire and motivate students of communication to be truthful in discharging their responsibilities has endured.

This edition includes an obituary of Mr. Chang written by one of his former students, Mr. C K Lau, former editor of the *South China Morning Post* and now associate dean of the School of Communication.

Many of Mr. Chang's students are accomplished professionals in the media industry and beyond. After he passed away in 2006, they worked with their alma mater and Mr. Chang's family to set up the Chang Kuo-sin Journalism and Communication Education Fund to honour and promote his legacy. They have also organised the Chang Kuo-sin Award for Aspiring Young Communicators to recognise budding journalists, commentators and film-makers who demonstrate the highest professional standards, exemplify the philosophy "truth is virtue" and display a high degree of originality.

On the centenary of Mr. Chang's birth, it is only fitting that we should republish *Eight Months Behind the Bamboo Curtain* to mark his tremendous contributions and achievements.

Last but not least, I would like to thank the Chang family for granting permission to reprint this book, the City University of Hong Kong Press for taking up the project and C K Lau, Robin Ewing and Patricia Chan for putting this edition together.

Professor HUANG Yu
Dean of School of Communication
Hong Kong Baptist University

Chang Kuo-sin –
Patriot Who Stuck to the Truth

In 1928, when 11-year-old Chang Kuo-sin and his father left their native Hainan Island in search of a better life in Kuching, North Borneo (now East Malaysia), he had only a rudimentary education in Chinese. The farm boy could not have dreamed that twenty years later, he would have mastered English and his coverage of the Chinese civil war would be read by millions all over the world. Nor would he have expected to become an unofficial emissary who attempted to alter the course of Sino-Indian relations, a film producer who entertained millions and a teacher who inspired generations. When the former head of the Communication Department of Hong Kong Baptist College (now Hong Kong Baptist University) passed away on February 2, 2006, he left a legacy that has few parallels. He was 89.

Chang was born on September 18, 1916, to a rural family at a time when China was still a sleeping giant and life for ordinary people was tough. In those days, in the coastal provinces of southern China, it was common for men to leave behind their families for better prospects in *nanyang*, a term that literally means the "south seas" and refers to a region now covered by Malaysia, Singapore and Indonesia. Chang's father found a job in a restaurant in Kuching, and as the eldest son, Chang followed him there. He was enrolled in St. Joseph's College, but soon had to quit because his father was not earning enough to support his studies. With the help of relatives, Chang was admitted to a school in Johor Bahru, north of Singapore, the next year. The teenager was already older than most of the students, but he made up for lost time by studying diligently and soon found himself advancing five grades to the same level as his peers. Chang fell in love with English and read countless books in the school library. By 1937, despite having to quit school for family reasons before getting his secondary diploma, he had already acquired good English skills that would serve him well.

Back in Kuching, Chang helped represent litigants who did not speak English in the local courts. By then, the Sino-Japanese War had broken out. He followed the war by listening to the BBC at night and recounted it to fellow Chinese the next morning. In 1938, Chang won a lottery that paid a handsome $275 in the local currency. The dutiful son sent $100 to his mother in Hainan and used another $100 to start a coffee shop with eight partners, installing his father as manager. When his father fell out with his partners, Chang opted to buy out the others with borrowed funds. A year later, the coffee shop had become a thriving business. He paid off his debts and sent for his mother, younger brother and sister to join him and his father in Kuching.

The young man could have settled for a life as a businessman, but his patriotic spirit urged him to return to China to help defend the nation. Chang's plan was to join the air force, but that was derailed by a chance encounter with Richard Wong, a young Chinese man who was returning from Hawaii to study in China. The two became such good friends that Wong, whose family was close to a senior Chinese official, helped Chang enroll in the National Southwestern Associated University. Based in Kunming in Yunnan province, the university was the war-time amalgamation of Peking, Tsinghua and Nankai universities. Fortunately for Chang, who had weak Chinese writing skills, the professors allowed him to take his admission tests in English. He was accepted as a provisional student and formally admitted to study political science a year later after passing more tests. At the university, Chang met his future wife Lucy, who was a student in the foreign languages department.

Two years later, Chang was taken ill and had to suspend his studies. While recovering, he was recommended for his good English skills and became a translator with the Allied Forces in India. Based in Kashmir, he helped sift through mail from Japanese-occupied territories in China to gather intelligence on the situation there. On returning to China, Chang resumed his studies. When he graduated in 1945, he joined the Central News Agency in Chungking (now Chongqing) as a reporter, and was soon sent to Nanking (now Nanjing), capital of the nationalist government. A year later, Chang was recruited by the American news agency United Press (now United Press International) to help cover the biggest news story at the time: the failed peace talks between the nationalists and the communists and the latter's progressive victories on the battlefield. In 1946, he covered the conclusion of the six agreements between the nationalists and the communists under the mediation of General George Marshall, US President Harry Truman's special representative sent to mediate the Chinese civil war. In December 1948, he reported Generalissimo Chiang Kai-shek's decision to step down, followed by the fall of Nanking on April 23, 1949.

Through his work, Chang got to know many senior nationalist and communist leaders. But he never allowed personal feelings to cloud his judgment and was determined, as a journalist, to expose the truth. Chang later learned that having exposed corruption in the nationalist government, he had been suspected of being a communist sympathiser and Chiang had wanted him dead. Fortunately, Chiang was dissuaded from ordering his death by advisers who knew Chang. In fact, despite having been at university at a time when most students were pro-communist, Chang was among a minority who felt communism was an ideal that would not work.

After the communist forces took control of Nanking, Chang was barred from reporting to the news agency. However, he continued to take notes of his observations on communist rule. When the time came for him to leave, he knew that his notes would not get past the censors. By what he described as a stroke of luck, he thought of a way of sneaking them out. "My idea, which to my delight proved to be a complete success, was to buy a Chinese dinner set – for 12 persons – of porcelain bowls, dishes and spoons and a big camphor chest. I packed the whole dinner set in the camphor chest using my notes as wrapping paper. The communist guards on several occasions looked into the camphor chest, but when they saw the dinner set wrapped in what they thought was merely used paper, they passed me on", he recounted later.

Arriving in Hong Kong in December 1949, Chang turned his notes into twenty-two pieces on life under communist rule in China for the United Press. The articles were distributed widely all over the world, and he was credited with being the first writer to use the term "bamboo curtain" to describe Chinese communist rule. He later expanded the articles into a book called *Eight Months Behind the Bamboo Curtain*. In the book, he observed that "the communists would have to change their ways or they would ultimately fail" and that "as communists, they would succeed, while their communism would not". He was happy to note, in 1999, that his observations had been confirmed by subsequent developments. "The Chinese communists have changed and they are still in power. They retain their name – communists – but have abandoned their communism", he said.

In 1952, with the support of the Ford Foundation, Chang founded Asia Press to publish the works of Chinese scholars who had left the mainland. Between 1952 and 1960, it published more than four hundred books, including novels, dramas, history and biography. In 1953, he went into film-making by launching Asia Pictures. Several of his films became big hits. *Long Lane* became the first Hong Kong film to win an award in the Asian Film Festival in 1956. Another film, *The Three Sisters*, released in the early 1960s when Hong Kong was ravaged by cholera, broke the box record for Mandarin Chinese films and catapulted actress Chang Chung Wen to stardom. The film's theme song, "Cha Shao Pao" (barbecue pork bun), which was adapted from the American hit "Hey Mambo", has become a classic. Its lyrics were written by Chang's wife Lucy.

In 1962, war broke out between China and India in the Himalayas. In Taiwan, Chiang Kai-shek regarded this as an opportunity to persuade New Delhi to switch diplomatic recognition from Beijing to Taipei. By then, Chang's work in Hong Kong had convinced Chiang that he was not a communist and could be trusted as his unofficial emissary. Chang secretly went to India, where he met with Prime Minister Jawaharlal Nehru, but the mission was unsuccessful. On the same trip, he also met the Dalai Lama, who had set up his government-in-exile in India after fleeing Tibet in 1959. In fact, Chang's friendship with the elder brother of the Dalai Lama dated back to his student days in Yunnan.

It was because of this secret mission to India, that Chang resigned as president of the Rotary Club of Hong Kong Island East, to the surprise of fellow Rotarians. He had been a veteran member, having joined the Rotary fellowship in Nanking in 1947, and many did not understand, even for some time after, why he resigned.

In 1968, Chang had a stint as editorial consultant with the *South China Morning Post*. Between 1971 and 1978, he wrote a weekly column, "A Chinese Viewpoint", for the paper. From 1976 to the 1990s, his column, "A Chinese Opinion", appeared in the *Hong Kong Standard*. Chang's writings were widely cited for his insight. In 1973, he correctly concluded from reading the article "Confucius the Man" in the *People's Daily* that it was an attack on Chinese Premier Chou En-lai. Chang was also author of *A Survey of the Chinese*

Language Daily Press (1968) and *Mao Tse-tung and His China* (1978).

When Hong Kong Baptist College started its communication programme in 1968, founding head Professor Timothy Yu asked Chang to help teach feature writing as a part-time lecturer. This later turned into a full-time position, as he also taught press law, political science and reporting on China. At a time when China was closed to the outside world, Chang's reporting on China class generated a lot of interest. Drawing on his extensive network, he was able to invite many veteran journalists and diplomats with experience in China to talk to his students. In 1978, Chang became head of the Communication Department and later, dean of the Faculty of Social Science. In the early 1980s, he played a critical role in overseeing the successful validation of the communication programme by the United Kingdom's Council for National Academic Awards. This paved the way for the programme's eventual recognition by the Hong Kong Government as being on a par with an honours degree programme.

In 1985 and 1986, Chang taught at the Ohio University's E.W. Scripps School of Journalism in Athens, Ohio, as an exchange professor. Students at Ohio liked him so much that the university asked him to stay on as an associate professor, which he did, even though he had retired from Hong Kong Baptist College in 1986. In 1988, when he was already 74, he decided to retire for the last time and the university gave him a wooden rocking chair, a gift usually awarded only to tenured professors.

On account of his fatherly appearance and strict but affable nature, Chang was known to his students as "Lo Yeh", an affectionate term meaning a venerable patriarch. "I still recall his lovely gesture of sitting back and laughing cutely, with one hand smoothing his grey hair, when he was talking about something funny or humorous", remembers Wong Ling-ling, one of his students. An oft-repeated remark by Chang in class was about communism: "When you're 18 and you're not a communist, you're a fool. When you're 48 and you're still a communist, you're also a fool". Although Chang was not fond of communism, that did not mean he was opposed to all communist thought. Another former student, Lo Wai-luk, recalls getting full marks for a piece on the future of communism in China after the fall of the Gang of Four. "I do not agree with your views, but your logic is good and your English is not bad. You've made an effort and I'll give you full marks", Lo quotes Chang as saying.

Chang felt strongly that all those who work in mass communication, be they in journalism, film-making, advertising or public relations, must have a solid grounding in reporting. He insisted that all communication students, regardless of their major, take news writing and reporting courses before focusing on their specialised studies. Above all, they must stick to the truth. He made "truth is virtue" the motto of the Communication Department. In 1981, when the Sing Tao Communication Building was built with donations from then *Sing Tao Daily* owner Sally Aw, he had the motto inscribed onto a marble plaque at the entrance.

For adhering to the truth, Chang was blacklisted by the nationalists and the communists at different times, but that did not stop him from speaking out. Nor did he alter his views when both sides tried to win him over. In the 1970s, Chang went on an officially arranged tour of Taiwan and was accompanied by Chiang Kai-shek's son, Chiang Ching-kuo, who later became president. He was impressed by Taiwan's economic success but not its political suppression. In 1984, he went to mainland China for the first time since 1949 at the invitation of the government. He was happy that the communists were changing their ways, but he did not like everything he saw. On both occasions, he expressed his feelings in his writing.

In retirement, Chang settled in the United States, where most of his children now reside. In his final years, he lived in Sacramento, California, but came back to Hong Kong every now and then. Each time he was back, he was feted by his former students, who all have fond memories of how "Lo Yeh" exhorted them to stick to the truth and strive for the best.

Chang is survived by his wife, two sons, three daughters, their spouses and five grandchildren.

LAU CK
Associate Dean, School of Communication
Hong Kong Baptist University
Former Editor, *South China Morning Post*
First written in 2006
Revised in 2016

Preface to the First Edition

This book is written on the advice and persuasion of newspaper readers and friends who thought that the twenty-one articles I wrote for the United Press when I arrived here in Hong Kong on December 23, 1949 were the first comprehensive and systematic reports on the Chinese communists that had ever come out of Red China. They suggested that the articles be expanded into a book for the information of the world in general and the Chinese overseas in particular.

I acknowledge that this book tells only part of the story of China's new rulers. It is not a story of my life in Red China, but a report on my observations on communist rule, on how it affected the common man, and how the common man in China felt towards it during the eight months I was behind the Bamboo Curtain.

It is not a scholastic study of the present and future of the Chinese communists. It is not history, but the facts which I give in this book will, I hope, help future historians in their work. The conditions and popular reactions which I report in this book are what existed during the period from

April 23 to December 23, 1949. They may change as time goes by, as they have changed before.

This book consists of two parts: (1) the communist "liberation" and administration of Nanking, the nationalist capital, and how the communists went about erecting their rule and how the people reacted towards them during the first month of occupation; and (2) the conditions and popular reactions throughout China after eight months of communist rule.

I added the first part for the purpose of showing the reader the difference in the tenor of popular reactions towards the Chinese communists after the people had been subjected to it for one month and subsequently eight months.

The difference, as the reader will discern, is that the people reacted favourably towards the Chinese communists after one month, but their reactions became unfavourable as time went by. This is true of all places in China. The change in popular reaction is one of the most significant phenomena, which to my knowledge has not yet been adequately publicised in the outside world.

As I said, this book is an objective report on communist rule in China as the common man sees it. If it is anti-communist in the final analysis, it is unintentional and something which I cannot help. As a correspondent, I must follow the popular trends.

I apologise to the reader for being unable to identify my sources as clearly as I should, as it may endanger the safety of my sources who are still living in China.

In illustration of the reasons of why we correspondents must be very careful in identifying our sources: one day our Shanghai correspondent met an American missionary in the streets and asked him about conditions in his area. He said he could not talk due to fear of communist reprisals. He said the communists had somehow gotten hold of an article in an American magazine which contained a description of conditions regarding missionaries in his area. The communists had then conducted a check of all the missionaries in the area in an effort to ascertain who had given the information to the writer.

I wish to thank Mr. Victor Kendrick, Chief United Press Staff Correspondent in Hong Kong, and Mr. Christopher Rand, *New York Herald Tribune* Correspondent in the Far East, for their suggestions and assistance in editing the manuscripts.

CHANG Kuo-sin
April 1950
Hong Kong

Preface to the Second Edition

My basic motivation in republishing this little book from a manuscript written forty-nine years ago (which was published in Chinese the same year) is to preserve a memento of my old days with the United Press of America, an experience that I value tremendously in my life.

I was the United States Staff Correspondent in China from 1946 to 1952, based in Nanking, the nationalist capital of China. When the Chinese communists banned foreign news agencies in the fall of 1949, I was transferred to the United Press Bureau in Hong Kong.

The original manuscript for this book was made for publication in Chinese. I must have kept copies but have lost them in the long years since and had not expected to see any copies until this one was found among the wartime papers of US General Claire L. Chennault.

General Chennault achieved fame when he organised the American Volunteer Group (AVG), also known as the Flying Tigers, in 1941 to aid China in the war against Japan. It was later expanded into the US 14th Air Force, and General Chennault became its commander with the rank of Lieutenant General.

This little book has no contemporary interest, albeit perhaps some contemporary relevance since it is possible that what the Chinese communists encountered and experienced in the first eight months of their rule might have helped convert them into what they are today.

The Chinese communists can be said to have been tamed at birth, the cumulative result being: the Chinese communists were compelled to abandon the radicalism of their Marxist ideology and continue to accept the moderation of Chinese philosophy, though stubbornly keeping their brand name – communism. They answered in their own way the question of what is in a name: as long as they keep their name, they could and are willing to do anything else.

At the end of my eight months stay behind the Bamboo Curtain, I left China with mixed feelings – with regret that I would not be able to witness what could be described as one of China's most cataclysmic transformations in history; and with happiness that moving to Hong Kong would assure my family and me a life without uncertainty and fear, where we could at least be sure of tomorrow.

In 1956, I met veteran journalist K.S. Chang in Singapore who gave me the first hint of what might have happened to me if I had stayed behind in China. His initials are the same as mine, leading the Chinese communists to mistake him for me. Mr. Chang was formerly editor-in-chief of the English-language *China Times* in Shanghai and moved to Singapore before the "liberation" to become the editor-in-chief of the *Singapore Standard*, often called the *Tiger Standard*. His wife, who was still in Shanghai when the city was "liberated", was denied an exit visa to join her husband in Singapore. The Chinese communists thought she was my wife. After they realised their mistake, they granted her the exit visa. The Chinese communists continued their pursuit of me, harassing and questioning some of my friends about my whereabouts.

In China I had watched and covered its greatest intellectual and political revolution in history. I learned much about the forces of history which alienated the government from the people and inspired a revolution to establish democracy and freedom. I learned, too, that all good things do not always end in good results.

The Chinese communist revolution to overthrow autocracy and oppression ended, as we all know by now, in worse democracy and oppression. That was what appeared in the first eight months of communist rule in China. But it has changed over the years and has become more acceptable to the Chinese people.

In my 1950 manuscript, I reported copiously on the negative Chinese public reactions to communist rule –

cynical, sceptical and even sometimes belligerent. I observed that the Chinese communists would have to change their ways or they would ultimately fail and also that, as communists, they would succeed, while their communism would not.

These two observations seemed to have been amply justified by subsequent developments. The Chinese communists have changed and they are still in power. They retain their name – communists – but have abandoned their communism.

Although I had not predicted the Soviet-Chinese communist split in 1960, I had concluded from the negative public reactions that the two communist countries could not stay ideological allies for too long. The split, however, is to be expected as a logical conclusion of the obvious Chinese people's rejection of Soviet Russia as China's "Big Brother", as she had been portrayed by Chinese communist propaganda.

When the time came for my family and me to leave China for Hong Kong, my biggest problem was how to sneak out the volumes of notes I had taken during my stay behind the Bamboo Curtain so that I could use them for my reports. In a moment of enlightenment or in a stroke of luck, I thought of a way to do so and hence embarked on my long journey from Shanghai.

My idea, which to my delight proved to be a complete success, was to buy a Chinese dinner set for twelve persons of porcelain bowls, dishes and spoons and a big camphor chest. I packed the whole dinner set in the camphor chest using my notes as wrapping paper. The communist guards on several occasions looked into the camphor chest, but when they saw the dinner set wrapped in what they thought was merely used paper, they waved me through.

During my trip from Shanghai to Hong Kong I avoided as far as possible revealing my identity as an "imperialist running-dog" correspondent. Only on two occasions was I compelled to reveal my identity, but to my surprise the communist guards became more polite to me.

The guards did not know that I was carrying volumes of notes I had made in the eight months behind the Bamboo Curtain on what had happened after the communists took over and my observations on what had happened between the communists and the people. I knew that I had to write these notes of my experiences when caught behind the Bamboo Curtain – a region closed to the outside world; the United Press surely expected this of me. I had worried a lot about how to get the notes out of China because I knew that if I were caught I would be charged with being a spy.

When taking the notes, I made three sets of them. Apart from the set I sneaked out in the camphor chest, I sent one set by mail to Hong Kong from Shanghai and one set from Canton. The set from Canton arrived five months later, while the set from Shanghai never arrived. The camphor chest set was the only set I had on arrival in Hong Kong and they gave me the data to write the twenty-one articles for the United Press. These articles were widely used and became what were called the first inside reports from behind the Bamboo Curtain.

I wish to thank my granddaughter Jennifer Nee-wah Kim for editing the original manuscript for republication in this book. She has done a great job in putting things in an orderly manner. For this I shall be forever grateful.

CHANG Kuo-sin
December 1999
Sacramento, California

EIGHT MONTHS BEHIND THE BAMBOO CURTAIN

PART ONE

Communists Rule in Nanking
After One Month of Trial
(April 23 – May 23, 1949)

I began my life behind the Bamboo Curtain on April 23, 1949, the day the nationalists pulled out of Nanking. "Bamboo Curtain" is a term coined by the American press for the totalitarian rule which the Chinese communists are expected to establish in China.

"Bamboo Curtain", in my opinion, is a more appropriate term for China than "Iron Curtain", which is used in reference to Soviet Russia, because the barrier against the outside world would not be as tight as that erected by Soviet Russia, due to the long vulnerable Chinese coastline and the large Chinese population abroad.

Another meaning of the Bamboo Curtain is that people behind a bamboo curtain can see outside the curtain, but people outside cannot see inside. This is generally presumed to be what the Chinese communists and communists in other countries are doing – banning foreign observation and inspection of their country, while maintaining a gigantic information or espionage network in other countries.

The most remarkable thing that emerged after the "liberation" of Nanking was the ingenuity and scale of the communist underground network. The set-up of the nationalist political and economic nerve centre was infested with the virus of communist espionage and sabotage, covering every part and level of the governmental machinery and reaching deep even into the Army Headquarters. This was one of the causes of the fast disintegration of Chiang Kai-shek's power.

One communist underground agent told me there were eight thousand underground workers in Nanking. He said three thousand of them were members of the Communist Party. Others were members of anti-Kuomintang parties and factions, communist sympathisers, individual political opportunists and people who were disgusted with the Kuomintang government. His figure may be a little exaggerated, but in my opinion it is pretty near to the truth.

Some of the underground agents were high up and deep in the most vital and confidential branches of the nationalist government. Some started their career in the civil service immediately after they left college and after going through the normal spell of training set up by the Kuomintang. Little wonder that all the secrets of the nationalist government were known to the communists before they were locked in the safety box. In Nanking, whenever the Garrison Headquarters drew up a blacklist of names for a nocturnal police round-up, the communist underground always had the list before the police were informed of it.

During the peace negotiations in Peking in April 1949, nationalist peace delegate General Liu Fei insisted to chief communist peace delegate Chou En-lai, now Premier of the Central People's Government, that the nationalist army totalled over four million men and could still fight if the communists refused to accede to their peace proposals.

Premier Chou En-lai smiled and took a piece of paper from his drawer and showed it to General Liu. That piece of paper contained the most detailed information on the disposition of all the remaining nationalist units with the names of even the battalion commanders. The paper gave the total strength of the remnant nationalist army as 1.1 million. General Liu, according to the communist sources who gave me the story, "reddened with embarrassment" and said, "Well, our payroll shows over four million men".

After the nationalist army pulled out of Nanking, communist underground agents immediately revealed their identity and quietly went on to take over governmental offices and property. The chief reporter, Mr. Li Kuo, and several typesetters in the Kuomintang party organ, *Central Daily News*, announced their identity in a meeting of the paper's staff on April 23 and formed a committee for checking and taking over the paper's plant. In the Central News Agency, eight members of its staff emerged as communists.

Two editors of the Military News Agency (operated by the Nationalist Defence Ministry), who had access to all of the war and intelligence reports of the Ministry's G-2 Department, turned out to be members of Marshal Li Chi-sen's Kuomintang Revolutionary Committee.

Even the confidential secretary of the Chief of G-3 Department of the Nationalist Defence Ministry, Captain Huang, was a communist. He had obtained his commission after a period of training in a Kuomintang military academy and was given the important position because of his "loyal" service.

As the confidential secretary of the G-3 Chief, Captain Huang handled all of the top-secret documents concerning military operations, defence plans, and troop deployment. When the Defence Ministry was making preparations to move out of Nanking a few days before the fall of the city, he quit the Ministry – but not before stealing top-secret military maps of defence works and strategic areas in Taiwan.

At the end of May 1949, I wrote a series of six articles for the United Press on how communist rule had affected the common man in Nanking after a period of one month.

These six articles are reproduced here without any change as the first portion of my report on communist rule.

1. Communist Government

The communists have set up a skeletal, but efficient and lenient administration in Nanking; yet, communist occupation has thrown the city into a mild business depression and serious unemployment problem.

Despite the fact that the nationalists tore down the municipal government and police force when they left – obviously to make things difficult for their enemies – the communists with efficiency and thoroughness have now succeeded in restoring all of the city's municipal and public services.

Communist leniency shown here is in conformity with their so-called "Eight Contractual Laws", their basic policy of city administration which is based on the principles of maintaining economic status quo and clemency towards past anti-communist political activities.

Persuasion, not pressure, is used in bringing the "unorthodox" to the line of communist thinking. Even former Kuomintang secret service men are allowed freedom, albeit apparently under close surveillance.

Foreigners here fare better than those in Peiping or Tientsin. They enjoy the advantage of official contact with the communists who have set up a foreign affairs department headed by Yenching graduate Huang Hua to attend to their troubles, if any.

Their property has not been violated and there are no restrictions imposed on their movement even to city suburbs. Initial anti-foreign actions taken by individual communist soldiers – such as the unconventional entry into US Ambassador John Leighton Stuart's residence – were halted promptly by order of the Communist High Command.

Foreign diplomatic missions ran into their first major difficulty with the communists over the re-registration of automobiles and telephones. The communists, maintaining that they have not established diplomatic relations, refuse – as in Peiping and Tientsin – to recognise the international law status of the missions and require them to re-register cars, telephones, and names of individuals, though property actually belongs to their respective governments. The matter is still in negotiation.

The first concrete benefit of communist rule here is relative economic stability. Prices of imported and manufactured articles are much higher than before but essential daily needs such as rice, cooking oils and meat are enjoying a stability previously unseen. According to a Nanking University survey, the general cost of living index this month has risen only about forty percent, which appears negligible compared with the doubling daily in skyrocketing inflation under the Kuomintang. The communist *renminbi* currency depreciated about sixty percent during the same period.

However, business has hit a mild depression. This is a natural result of the nationalist abandonment of Nanking as their capital, where former business prosperity thrived chiefly on the heavy concentration of purchasing power inherent in the city's political position as the seat of the national government.

The business decline is best illustrated in the words of a barber who told me, "I cut the hair of more than ten persons daily before, but now only one or two persons". The general shopkeeper, tailor, restaurant owner, and mechanic talk similarly.

2. Popular Reactions

Chiang Kai-shek, the Generalissimo, the President and the Kuomintang Tsungtsai, is now "Chiang the Bald Head" and "Chiang the Country Betrayer" in Nanking, the seat of his power since 1927.

This propaganda smear against the retired Chinese president is carried to the population in slogans and political lectures. The Nanking communist organ *New China Daily* published a short poem captioned "Chiang the Bald Head" which is taught even to primary school children.

This is part of a well-organised propaganda campaign, carried out here by communist political workers and assisted enthusiastically by students, to proselytise ideologically the Nanking populace which has been fed with anti-communist propaganda for a longer time than those of other cities.

Communist underground workers and students posted slogans even before communist troops entered the city on April 24. One caricature depicted Chiang Kai-shek with five human skulls in his belly showing how he had "eaten up" the people. Most slogans attacked Kuomintang misgovernment.

One of the most popular posters demanded the confiscation of the bureaucratic capital of China's big four families: the Chiangs, Soongs, Kungs and Chens. The *New China Daily* reported their total wealth is sufficient "to supply rice for the world's population for thirty-two months, the Chinese population for twelve years; clothe the world's poor for thirteen years, China's for 680 years; purchase 2.2 billion ounces of gold; build 110,000 hospitals averaging one to every four thousand Chinese; and build eleven million schools in China".

A chief part of the "ideological proselytism" drive is the so-called "learning movement", that is, learning the "new knowledge" consisting mainly of Marxist and Leninist theories, Mao Tse-tung's "New Democracy" and "On Coalition Government" and Yangko dance and songs.

"Learning" meetings are held daily among the students, workers, and other types of people. They are organised by communist political workers, or even by the participants themselves.

The "ideological proselytism" drive appears to have achieved considerable success. Communist political theories, Kuomintang misgovernment and Mao Tse-tung's political programme for China are now the main topics in private conversations. The Yangko dance is performed in schools, homes and the streets and its songs are hummed everywhere in the town. Mao Tse-tung's two booklets, "New Democracy" and "On Coalition Government", are best sellers in the town.

The populace here displaces a remarkable sense of security under the communists. The former feeling of tension appears to have given place to one of general contentment, stemming presumably from the widespread belief that with the communist occupation the civil war is over as far as this city is concerned.

The communists were getting a good start in their effort to win over support here by the public felicitous mood which resulted from the quick conclusion of the Battle of Nanking. Many had expected the battle to be drawn out and the city beleaguered for some time and had hoarded a few months' supply of rice.

There are still people who maintain their anti-communist views and people who look askance at the communists. For instance, some businessmen are adopting a wait-and-see attitude before resuming operations with their former vigour. One businessman told me, "We are now hesitant of earning big money because we are unsure if the money we earn with our sweat will remain ours in the future".

However, indications show that people as a whole are inclined to accept the communists as their new government. A large section of the populace has displayed even more than the inclination to accept; but students and workers, who constitute the backbone of Chinese urban society, are more enthusiastic in welcoming the communists.

There are definitely more people who welcome the communists than those who regret the departure of the nationalists. Even the complainants I talked to do not wish for the return of the nationalists. The farthest they would go is to hope that the communists would modify their policies to suit their individual interests.

The favourable popular reactions to the communist rule here are generally ascribed by competent observers to three factors: (1) the relative economic stability they have brought in; (2) their well-behaved and disciplined army;

and (3) the popular conviction that with their arrival the civil war is over, permitting the revival of long-lost political security.

It is noted that it is only natural these factors have made such an impact on the psychology of the masses who were plagued by civil war and undisciplined soldiery during the last few decades and by a nightmarish inflation in the last three years. By habit they assess a system on the basis of its actual effects on their daily lives, rather than on its theoretical merits.

The broader international and political complications of the situation – one of the main worries of Western democracies – are absent from their minds. Communist political and theoretical influence is strong, sometimes even more so among the educated class.

3. Communist Press

Communist rule has created a news hunger in Nanking. The majority of the people I talked to in my survey of popular reactions to the communists complain, "There is no news to read nowadays".

Two of them – a gasoline seller and a shop assistant – asked me if they could subscribe to the United Press news service. I told them we do not and perhaps never will distribute news in Nanking. To this the gasoline seller persuaded, "But I would buy your service only for personal reference". I replied, "Sorry, even that we cannot do".

The news hunger is not the outcome of the decreased number of newspapers in the town but a result of the kind of news they had been accustomed to reading before the communists came no longer being available, namely, human interest and social stories such as divorces, crimes, reports on the activities and meetings of high officials, and foreign agency despatches on the China situation.

At present, only two vernaculars serve the estimated 1.1 million population of Nanking: the communist organ *New China Daily* and the privately owned but pro-communist *China Daily*. Another privately owned paper, the *Hsinminpao*, which was banned by the Kuomintang, is reported to have obtained communist permission to resume publication shortly. The other seventeen papers have been ordered to suspend publication pending registration with the communist military control commission.

The New China and the China dailies print only Communist New China News Agency despatches and some Tass reports on the international situation, and occasionally one or two other short foreign agency items. Their content is mainly propagandist, educative, and literary in nature, e.g., Communist Party declarations, editorials, propaganda features and lengthy stories on production, political activities, and meetings of workers and students.

Because only one news distribution source is available, the papers contain practically the same information. Buying one paper is sufficient and after buying the morning paper it is usually unnecessary to buy the evening paper because it often prints the same material as its morning contemporaries.

One newspaper executive told me that under these conditions the future of journalistic developments in China will be extremely limited. During the first three weeks of communist occupation, when old newspapers were allowed to continue publication, their circulation rapidly declined because most people who used to buy more than one morning paper and people who used to buy both the morning and evening papers now bought only one, as one was sufficient to keep one abreast of all the printable news.

"Even if we were permitted to resume publication", the executive added, "it is exceedingly doubtful we could get enough circulation to keep ourselves out of the red". He observed that one or two thousand newspaper workers in Nanking were faced with the problem of *"chuang yeh"* (changing profession). The executive suggested one possible way out is to find a new type of reporting which would fulfil the requirements of both the communists and the reading public.

One veteran Chinese editor who had watched communist press operations in Peiping the last few months said, "Under the communists there is no news competition and the entire emphasis is placed on accuracy. Accuracy under the communists is both factual and political in meaning".

In the *New China Daily* a reader frequently comes across delayed stories. For instance, I saw a story of a discussion meeting presided over by Mayor Liu Po-chen which was held four days earlier. Upon inquiry I was told by a communist newspaperman the reason for this delay was that after the reporter had written his story he had to show it to everyone he had quoted to check if the quotes were correct.

Though there were no restrictions on the foreign press in the collection of news, none of the communist officials in town would receive us in a news-gathering visit. The reasons, according to a Chinese newspaperman, are: (1) the communist journalistic code discourages reporting on officials or official activities and enjoins that reportorial effort should be concentrated on the production and the life of the common man; and (2) an ordinary communist official is not free to talk. Every word he says to newspapermen must receive the prior approval of high authorities.

The communist journalistic code also is said to enjoin the publication of only the good things in ordinary social life. This accounts for the disappearance of reports on robberies, murders, and divorces in the communist press.

4. The Communist Army

The Liberation Army appears to be the trump card of the communists – it wins battles as well as popularity for them.

If you ask ten Chinese in a city newly-captured by the communists you will find nine of them starting off, "Oh, their army is really good and well-disciplined". Even people whom I know to still be anti-communist in their political views have admitted that the communist army is the best China has ever seen. I know of at least two friends who changed their views about the city's new rulers after they had seen more of the Red Soldiers.

A common observation in this town is that if Chiang Kai-shek were to have a similar chance of personal contact with the communist army, he might change his mind, too.

Communist soldiers have brought a new story into Nanking, though it is not possible to ascertain how true it is. The story, now widely circulated in the city, is that a nationalist soldier cannot meet his communist counterpart, as he will defect before the conversation is over.

The story also claimed there were many straying nationalist army men in the front trying to get back to their units running into straying communist soldiers. They stopped to talk with each other with the communists always starting off, "For whom are you fighting?" Invariably the result is, according to the story, the nationalist soldiers picked up their rifles and walked away in the opposite direction behind the communist soldiers.

From what I have seen of the communist soldiers in Nanking I found that they possess the following features which are never or very rarely evident in other Chinese soldiers:

They are well-mannered, polite and "chiang tao li" (talk reason). They say "please" and *"tui pu chi"* (sorry), and you can argue with them. With the nationalists, prudence frequently is the better side of valour when it comes to a dispute.

One day I watched several communist soldiers pleading patiently with some stall-keepers to move their stalls inner to the road along Chungcheng Street. They implored, "We are sorry, but please move your stalls inner. It's safer for you and more convenient for motor traffic". This is in sharp contrast to the way the nationalist gendarmes kicked down traffic-blocking stalls I saw before.

They have a high level of education. It cannot be ascertained what is the exact literacy percentage, but one noteworthy observation is that when they came into Nanking the best selling commodity in town was cheap Chinese-made fountain pens.

In political indoctrination, qualified observers granted them an easy one hundred percent. This is believed to be the main factor accounting for the high sense of confidence and fighting for a cause among the Liberation Army men.

They are well cared for medically. I learned that the Communist 35th Army, which was the first unit to enter Nanking and which originally was the Nationalist 84th Division which defected at Tsinan last year, has two thousand doctors and Liu Po-chen's general headquarters five thousand doctors. (Most of these doctors, however, are graduates of short-term courses.)

Dr. K.F. Yao, superintendent of the Central Hospital, said the level of medical education must be very high in the communist army. He noted that during the first two weeks of communist occupation a long stream of communist soldiers came to his hospital for a physical check-up and he had to set up a special clinic just to take care of them.

The pay scale in the communist army is lower than in the nationalist army, but their food is better and contains more meat. One novel piece of equipment in the communist army is a sausage-like bag about four feet and four inches in diameter containing rice and carried by the soldiers. It apparently is a guerrilla warfare necessity.

It is reported that the communists drill very little. Their chief training is walking, marching and shooting straight. The average communist soldier has little knowledge of the modern city facilities. One day the *New China Daily* reported that the soldiers were learning how to use the flush toilet, switch on electric lights, and turn on the water pipe.

5. Nationalist Retreat from Nanking

The nationalist retreat from Nanking, orderly at the beginning, degraded into an undisciplined, and in some phases, a panicky flight, leaving behind a backwash of bitterness and disrepute.

The general retreat began at four a.m. on April 24, the decision to abandon the capital having been made only seven hours earlier after the city's right and left flanks were turned by communist river-crossing operations.

Acting President Li Tsung-jen and Premier Ho Ying-chin returned to Nanking in the afternoon of April 22 from their meeting with Generalissimo Chiang Kai-shek at Hangchow with no thought of the contingency ever arising to evacuate the city next morning. They sneaked out of Nanking by plane one hour after the general retreat started.

Defeated soldiers maintained correct army discipline for a few hours and then started robbing, looting and "*la fu*" (forcing people to carry loads for them). Even now some people still talk bitterly of the way they had been robbed and "*la fu*". Alert communist propagandists took full advantage of the incorrect behaviour of the nationalist soldiers immediately when they entered the city on the morning of April 24. They pasted posters all over the town asking the people, "Have you seen them taking a needle or a piece of thread from the people? Compare them, please, with Chiang Kai-shek's rebels!"

The following are a few instances of nationalist "*la fu*" and robbery which came to my attention:

(1) A pedicab belonging to the Shanghai *Takungpao Daily* was taken away. The paper's jeep was also "requisitioned" and its driver was forced to drive nationalist soldiers to Tangshan, fifteen miles south of Nanking, where the dissolved American Joint Military Advisory Mission was once established. Only the driver was allowed to return from Tangshan.

(2) One Catholic-owned *Social Welfare Daily* reporter came across a nationalist soldier trying to rob a man of his bicycle. He broke in to mediate and settled it by giving the soldier the man's wristwatch.

(3) A United Press newsboy disappeared for four days and when he came back he said he was "*la fu*" up to Tangshan.

Robbery outside Nanking city by soldiers was said to be even worse. One popular singsong girl who left the city April 23 for Shanghai by bus returned two days later minus all her jewels, gold bars, and dresses. A detailed story of her misfortune was published in a Nanking evening paper later.

One of my friends, whose Nanking-bound train was halted at Chengkiang and who had to walk to Nanking, reached home two days later, robbed of everything except his pants and singlet. He said he tried to take detours to avoid the robbing soldiery but "there were soldiers all over the countryside".

Panic was said to have struck the retreating nationalists at the later stage. One bank employee who left Nanking for Shanghai April 23 by car went only as far as Chuyung, twenty-five miles southeast of Nanking. He said his car could go no further because the road bridges had been destroyed and the road itself was blocked by a concentration of over ten thousand nationalist soldiers. As he was trying to find a detour, word came that the communists had arrived, which in turn threw the nationalist concentration into panic. Soldiers scattered, fleeing in all directions. Later it developed that the advance communist unit consisted of twenty communist soldiers.

Retreating nationalist soldiers, gendarmes, and police fought a sanguinary battle at Tangshan among themselves wrestling for motored transportation. Police and gendarmes possessed the trucks which were loaded mostly with personal belongings. Soldiers argued that the trucks now should carry men instead of baggage. Police and gendarmes refused to discard the cargo and the battle ensued with a large number of casualties.

The communist army's fast marching ability was another factor injecting confusion into the nationalist retreat route. The communist force marched to Liyang, fifty-five miles southeast of Nanking, in two and a half days. A nationalist division from Nanking trudged to Liyang on the fourth day. The rested communists disarmed with little difficulty the fatigued nationalists.

6. Communists and Foreign Recognition

Foreign diplomatic opinion here believes the communists at present are not anxious for foreign recognition.

This, foreign diplomats explain, means that they would establish diplomatic relations when offered on a footing of complete equality and in a spirit of friendliness. However, they would not ask for it.

A talk I had with one communist worker seemed to confirm the belief that to the communists it is mainly a question of accepting, not requesting, recognition. The worker, replying to my question, said, "We will accept the recognition of any country if that country abandons its superiority complex and unequal treaties and rights".

An independent Chinese source who enjoyed intimate connections with top communist officials told me, "The communists have not yet given any serious thought to recognition. They are still concentrating their energy and effort on completing the liberation of all China and restoration of production in liberated areas".

The communists seem to be exercising extreme caution in the question of foreign recognition and approaching the issue with a spirit of nationalistic pride. As a rule the communists are unwilling to talk about the question even in private conversations. One source told me that they have been instructed not to talk with any outsider on foreign matters without proper authorisation.

Opinions thus far regarding the communist position towards foreign recognition mostly are conjectures. The only official word on the matter was found in communist army spokesman Li Tao's statement recently on the incident involving the British sloop *Amethyst*. He said:

> If any foreign government is willing to consider the establishment of diplomatic relations with us, it must sever all connections with the remaining power of the Kuomintang and withdraw its armed forces from China.

A *Takungpao* editorial throws some light on the question. The privately owned daily is considered best capable of reflecting the communist official attitude. Deducting from utterances made by Mao Tse-tung and Army spokesman Li Tao's statement, the editorial concludes that new China's foreign policy during this interim period is thus: "We want all foreign governments to respect new China's independent and equal status and they will not be allowed to encroach on our internal affairs. We will by our own efforts strive to build a new democratic country and will not be too anxious about the establishment of diplomatic relations with foreign governments. Foreign life and property, however, will be protected".

PART TWO

Communist Rule in China
After Eight Months of Trial
(April – December 1949)

About a week after the communists captured Nanking, the nationalists severed all telegraphic and mail communications with the "liberated areas", while the Chinese Radio Administration maintained its only international radio station in Shanghai. As Shanghai was still held by the nationalists, we in Nanking were completely cut off from communication with the outside world. This was my first taste of the Bamboo Curtain and the conditions of my one-month isolation in Nanking taught me firsthand what it really meant.

We had no contact with the outside and knew nothing of what was happening in the outside world. The only means left to us to get information about the outside world was the radio receiver, but very few people possessed one.

There were several newspapers in town, but their contents were mostly glorification of the communists or condemnation of the enemies of the communists and not news in the strict sense of the word to the common man in Nanking. While the newspapers sometimes gave us what we considered news reports on world events, but they informed us only when and of what the communists thought we should be informed – after the event happened and in a subjective manner.

The summer floods, which were generally considered to be the worst disaster in China since 1931, were reported once in a long while, but only then when such conditions as the communists deemed permissible. There was nothing in the papers about Yugoslavia's recognition of new China. The same held true with the nationalist port closure order. After some weeks the people came to know about these two events, but only after someone had heard the news on the radio and circulated it through the native grapevine.

The *Daily Tribune Evening News* in Shanghai was banned because it printed a short despatch on the nationalist blockade, even though it was printed a week after the blockade was imposed and was common knowledge throughout the outside world.

The British-owned *North China Daily News* in Shanghai was ordered to make a public apology to the communists for reporting the suspected mining of the Yangtse River mouth by the nationalists. The suspected mining was first reported by qualified river pilots who were intercepted by a nationalist gunboat at the river mouth and who on their return journey saw the gunboat zigzagging at the estuary throwing things overboard. The reported mining, though proved to be unfounded later, held up shipping in Shanghai for about a week and was considered headline news at that time. Not a word about it appeared in the communist-controlled Chinese press.

While the nationalists were still in Nanking, the newspapers carried many reports, mostly communist-originated, on what was happening in the communist areas. With the communists controlling Nanking we read no reports in the press about what was happening in the nationalist camp, except "condemnation" releases and war reports put out by the communists.

During the first month of communist rule in Nanking, we practically glued our ears to the radio nightly for up-to-date progress reports on the battle of Shanghai. The press in Nanking was reticent about the battle until about four days prior to the communist capture of the port city, when urgent despatches appeared on communist victories.

One incident occurred on the night of May 25, demonstrating the thick-headedness of Kuomintang propaganda. Earlier in the day, the communists reported their army had entered Shanghai. This was later corroborated by American press despatches we heard on *Voice of America*, which had become the most popular station among the news-hungry populace. Late at night, we tuned in to the Kuomintang's Chungking radio station, *Voice of China*, just to see what the nationalists had to say about the loss of Shanghai. The station read a Central News despatch from Canton saying that the Nationalist Legislative Yuan had passed a note of thanks to the gallant defenders of Shanghai for their victory against the communists and resolved also to send a mission to comfort the troops in Shanghai. My wife, who was at my side at that time, screamed, "What a joke!" That, I later learned, was not "jocular" enough. When I arrived in Shanghai three days after the communist capture, my Shanghai colleagues told me that the nationalists had staged a "victory parade" in the city on the evening of May 23, the day before they were driven out.

––––––––––

The communists showed an unfriendly attitude towards the foreign press from the beginning. Shortly after they entered Nanking I made many unsuccessful attempts to get in touch with their information officials. They refused to see me because I was an "imperialist running-dog" reporter. Some friends of the Chinese press who were received by communist political workers told me that I might be received as well.

One day I went with three other Chinese reporters to the communist headquarters at the New Life Movement Centre. After passing an exhaustive cross-examination by communist gate guards, we were led through many long lanes and corridors into a building where we were told to wait for a communist liaison officer. We waited for half an hour, which stretched into one and a half hours, but the communist liaison officer had yet to appear. I was getting a little impatient and wanted to leave, but the other reporters told me that I would be unable to leave without the permission of the guards. I looked around for the guards, but could not find them. After some time I found one guard and asked him if I could leave. I was told to wait. I waited for another fifteen minutes. The liaison officer still did not show up. I asked the guard if I could now leave, but was once again told to wait.

At this point I became a little suspicious. Friends had told me before that one of the communist practices is that when they detain people they tell them to "wait" because they can't say, "You are detained". Could this be that kind of "waiting"? After another fifteen minutes, I decided to leave in the way I had been accustomed to under similar circumstances. I chose the moment when the guard was out of sight and walked out without any trouble.

Subsequent personal experiences substantiated what my friends had told me about communist "waiting". One night my wife was stricken with an acute stomach ache after the curfew was already on. Her pain worsened and I decided to take her to the hospital. Friends had told me that communist soldiers did not even give safe conduct to sick people during curfew hours, so I asked my colleague Ned Chow to go out into the streets, find some communist guards and get their permission for sending my wife to the hospital.

Ned returned after ten minutes. He said he met one soldier, but the soldier could not give us permission ahead of time and told Ned to go back to look after the sick woman. Half an hour elapsed. My wife's pain became more acute. I sent Ned out again to plead with the soldiers for permission. After waiting an hour for Ned, who had still not returned, I decided to drive my wife to the hospital. We were stopped once on the way, but the soldiers permitted us to pass.

Early the next morning I was going to search for my missing colleague when a man came to me with a note from Ned. Ned wrote that he had been detained at a communist barracks about two hundred yards from my house. I went there immediately and saw Ned sitting glumly on a bench smoking his last cigarette.

I asked him what had happened. He said he had been stopped by a communist patrol that was hiding in the ditch and jumped on him. He told them our problem and asked for permission to send my wife to the hospital. The patrol leader said that he would have to see his company commander for permission. They took Ned to the barracks. The company commander was out. Ned was told to wait.

He waited for some time and then asked if he could go home. The soldiers said, "No, please wait". He asked again if he could go home, but the reply was always, "Please wait". So he waited till dawn. By dawn, the company commander had returned and curfew was over. Ned asked if he could go home. Again, "Please wait". So he wrote me that note.

I went straight in to see the company commander, who was fast asleep after curfew duty. We woke him up and I asked him why Ned was not allowed to go home. He said Ned had violated curfew regulations last night and he had to "wait" till the higher authorities said he could go home. Ned was made to "wait" for another three hours before the final okay came for his release. "Waiting" for detention, as I found out later, is one of the many euphemistic words the communists use. They also call their detention camps for Kuomintang workers in Nanking "educational centres".

I ran into my first "waiting" incident the day the communists entered Nanking. That day I drove to the Ming Palace airfield to see how many planes the nationalists had left behind in their hasty retreat. The communist guard who stopped me at the gate gave me permission to inspect the airfield. But when I was in the airfield, I was waved back and told to "wait" in the airfield office. The communist political worker came out and asked who I was and what I was doing in the airfield. I told him that I was a reporter and had gotten permission from the gate guard before I entered the airfield. I refrained from telling them that I was a reporter from an American agency, but one of my friends who was with me leaked out my agency. When the political worker heard the word "American" he became stern.

He asked me if I had been sent there by the American Government. I told him no and explained to him that the American United Press was not a government organisation and had nothing to do with the American government. He questioned me further in a roundabout way whether I had any connections with the American government. Then he told me to "wait". I was a little displeased. If they did not want me in the airfield, I would leave. I had not sneaked in. I asked the gate guard first, but all my arguments were in vain. I "waited" for half an hour and my anxiety subsided when the political worker came back and told me that I could go, but stressed to me that I must go back to where I came from.

This "go back to where you came from" is one of the rules in the communist army manual, I later found out. When the communists came into Nanking, they did not announce a night curfew until about three weeks later. During the first three weeks, however, the street guards imposed their own unofficial curfew which started at different hours of the night. Many people, thinking there was no curfew because one had not been announced, were stopped when they went out into the streets. They argued with the soldiers that there was no curfew, as a curfew must be announced officially. They got nowhere with the soldiers, but they were not arrested. The soldiers just told them to "go back to where you came from". The trouble was that some had come from the movie house and had to spend the rest of the night at the theatre. The communist soldiers did the same thing in Shanghai when they took over the city, but people lodged complaints and soon they ceased.

In Shanghai during my first post-liberation visit, I was personally involved in a "go back to where you came from" incident. I had arrived in Shanghai three days after the communist capture and was out in the streets during the first few nights without anyone stopping me. One night I was returning from a party at a friend's house with two other foreign correspondents. We drove through the streets without incident until we arrived at the Garden Bridge on the Bund. There we were stopped by a communist solider. He told us to "go back to where we came from" because it was curfew hour.

Being the only Chinese-speaking member of the party, I argued with the soldier, but to no avail. A little ahead we saw a passenger-packed streetcar also being stopped. I told the soldier there was no official announcement of the curfew. He said he did not know if there were any official announcement, but his instructions were to enforce a curfew. I pointed to the well-illuminated Broadway

Mansions at the other side of the bridge and said that was where we lived and we must go there.

After arguing with the soldier for fifteen minutes, he told us, "Why are you so stubborn? If you can't go through this street, why don't you try other streets?" I wiped the beads of sweat from my forehead and we alighted from the car in search of an alternate street.

We walked into the next street and were stopped again. This soldier, unlike his comrade in the previous street, stopped only pedestrians, but not people riding in cars or pedicabs! I started the argument all over again. We were joined by other pedestrians and ganged up in a mass protest. The soldier finally agreed to ask his company commander for instructions. He went through several dark lanes to find his superior officer, who was presumably hiding himself in some dark corner, and came back ten minutes later saying we could go.

The communists began the offensive against Shanghai on May 18, 1949, and captured it on May 25. It was only in Shanghai that the nationalists put up any real fight south of the Yangtse River. In other places, it was merely walking over and in for the communists.

It was also in Shanghai that the communists suffered their greatest losses since the Manchuria collapse. General

Chen Yi, commander of the Communist Third Field Army, admitted in a private conversation with "democratic personages" (a pro-leftist who is not a Party member) in Shanghai that communist casualties in the Shanghai battle were over twenty-five thousand. General Chen said that at one stage of the battle he had to divert reinforcements from as far as southern Kiangsi.

The communists could have walked into Shanghai if they had started the attack immediately after they crossed the Yangtse River towards the end of April. But they bypassed Shanghai and lunged down to Hangchow, giving the routed nationalists under General Tang En-po two valuable weeks for regrouping and getting reinforcements from Taiwan.

Communist sources in Nanking later disclosed that the attack was delayed because the preparations for taking over Shanghai were incomplete. These sources said that the Communist High Command's estimation of Shanghai was that its capture militarily was easy, but administratively it was a problem. If they captured and administered it successfully, it would be the consolidation of their rule in China. If not, it could be the beginning of their failure in China.

Communist intelligence reports from Shanghai also said that the populace were unconcerned regarding their impending "liberation" by the communists because they were feeling as confidently as before that they could "Shanghainise" the communists as they had done to previous conquerors of the city.

Therefore, the sources added, the Communist High Command took the greatest care in preparing for taking over the administration in the port city. Later on I learned that a force of eighteen thousand communist workers was sent into Shanghai following the military capture for the restructuring, the largest administrative force ever assembled by the communists for taking over a city.

The Communist High Command's estimation of Shanghai appears to have been substantiated by current conditions. If the communists cannot curb the present inflation, speculation, hoarding and the active nascent political opposition and revive the stagnant industries and business in Shanghai, it may really prove to be a very serious threat to the stability of communist power in China.

The following chapters are a collection of the twenty-one articles I wrote for the United Press after I arrived in Hong Kong from China on December 23, 1949. I have expanded the articles with additional materials and data which I was unable to put into the originals because of space limitations.

The reader will find that the popular reactions to communist rule as reported in Part One of this book are more favourable to the communists than what I had reported in the following articles. This has become a pattern of popular reactions in China.

In practically all places the people clamoured for the communists before they came. After they came the people were jubilant over the good discipline of the communist army and the efficiency and honesty of their administration, but after the people had been subjected to communist rule for several months they became disillusioned with the communists.

1. Communist Totalitarianism

As a prerequisite to their ultimate aim of creating a totalitarian China, the Chinese communists have embarked on a programme of controlling thought and action:

Control of the press, publications, and education. Communist policy is to have only one press in China – the official press; though for reasons of political expediency, a few privately owned newspapers are permitted. Prominent among these are the *Takungpao* and the *Hsinminpao*. These papers, however, have communists in their editorial chairs.

Under the new ideology the communists' own newspapers, such as the *People's Daily* in Peking and the

Emancipation Daily in Shanghai, are the people's papers. Since only one paper is sufficient to serve the needs of the people, other kinds of papers are unnecessary.

In theory, the communists permit a free press and the freedom of factual reporting and criticism, but in actual practice the press is rigidly controlled to serve their political purpose, even at the sacrifice of factual reporting.

The following are two examples of communist suppression of the truth to serve their political purpose:

(1) The Chinese river steamer S.S. *Kiangling* was sunk on July 30, 1949, by communist shore artillery which was directed at the escaping British frigate H.M.S. *Amethyst*. This was according to the surviving crewmen and passengers of the ship. But the communist release said that the passenger-loaded ship was sunk by the *Amethyst*.

(2) On June 9, 1949, Shanghai river pilots reported that they saw two nationalist gunboats zigzagging at the South Channel Entrance of the Shanghai harbour and suspected mines had been laid. The pilots made a report to the communist authorities, who held daily conferences to discuss what should be done to determine whether the South Channel was actually mined. They arrived at no decision. Finally, the pilots, all foreigners, borrowed a motorboat from the

British Consulate and swept the Channel for the suspected mines. None were found.

The communists put out releases that the mining of the Yangtse River mouth was a rumour fabricated by reactionaries and imperialists. One paper which reported that the channel was swept of the suspected mines with foreign aid was punished.

The newspaper, in the eyes of the communists, is a vital political weapon. Chinese reporters working on communist papers said that the difference between reporting under the communists and in the democratic West is that under the communists the reporter has first to find a political purpose and then go out to gather news and write it in such a way as to promote that political purpose.

The freedom of the newspaper and other kinds of public criticism, permitted theoretically by the communists, are strangled in practice by the requirement that the criticism must be "constructive", that the critic must have good intentions and a thorough understanding of the problem before he speaks his mind. This requirement is open to varied interpretations.

Communist regulations announced in Nanking and Shanghai contain no provision that can be considered an insurmountable obstacle against the registration of privately owned papers, except the provisions that the newspaper should not print anything prejudicial to the interests of the people, the principles of Chairman Mao Tse-tung's New Democracy and the law of the people's government. Many newspaper executives would be ready to meet this requirement if only they were permitted to publish a paper. But to obtain permission to publish a paper in Red China is now impossible.

Under conditions created by the communists, it is also impossible for privately owned papers to exist. Newspaper publishing has always been a losing business in China. During the Kuomintang days, newspapers had little difficulty in getting some politically minded rich men to finance them. They were also given assistance by the government in the form of controlled-price newsprint.

Moreover, the contents of newspapers today are tightly controlled by the communists to serve their propaganda and the contents consequently are similar and appeal very little to the reader, which cuts down circulation. Therefore, even if someone is permitted to publish a newspaper he may have to close in a short time due to small circulation. The *China Times* in Nanking, which was allowed to continue publication by the communists, shut down for this reason. Excepting a few privately owned publications, all other newspapers and magazines, including those which had pursued a pro-communist editorial policy during the Kuomintang days were banned.

The popular pro-communist *Observer* weekly in Shanghai was permitted to resume publication only after two months of arduous negotiations. One of the communist conditions was that the weekly's editorial office be shifted to Peking to ensure proficient communist control. The publisher was also required to set up a seven-man editorial committee, consisting of communist-trusted people, to examine the articles before they were printed.

The *Takungpao*, formerly known as the best Chinese independent daily, is also now under communist control. One of the changes the communists made in the paper's traditional editorial policy is to print New China News Agency editorials on the front page. The old editorial staff resisted this change, but to no avail. Only the news service of the New China News Agency and the Soviet Tass Agency are made available to the newspapers. Consequently, their contents are similar every day.

Publication of books is now virtually a state monopoly in the hands of the Communist New China Book Publishing Company. There are several privately owned publishing companies, but like the privately owned newspapers, they are controlled by the communists. The New China Company now has 375 branches. A plan has been mapped out to expand the Company to the extent of having one branch in every city in China.

Education is controlled through the appointment of teachers and professors and the alteration of the curriculum even for primary schools. In universities, Mao Tse-tung's New Democracy, the history of social development and Marxist dialectics are compulsory courses even for engineering students. The English translation of Mao Tse-tung's July 1st speech on "the People's Democratic Dictatorship" is now the first lesson in freshman English.

Communist control in this field is so rigid that in areas where communist rule has been firmly established no one can now teach or write or publish as he sees fit, or express his personal opinions in any other public way without the approval of the communists. As a result, the communist freedom of expression is described as the freedom to praise but not to criticise.

Regimentation of social life. This is being achieved through the organisation of many national and local societies and the reorganisation of existing ones, the membership of which covers all walks of life and ages. They are designed to herd every Chinese into some sort of a state-controlled body.

Children, when they are nine years old, may enter the Children's Corps, where they remain until they are sixteen years old. They may then join the "new democracy" Youth Corps. After the Youth Corps, they are regimented into the association of the profession which has been chosen for their livelihood.

The communists are laying special emphasis on the labour unions. House servants are also organised into unions and even business guilds are being gradually brought under control. In places where the regimentation of social life has been carried out to an advanced stage, it is virtually impossible for a man who is not a member of one of the state-controlled organisations to earn a living.

Political indoctrination. This is the policy into which the communists are presently putting most of their energy – in their eyes its success is essential to the consolidation of communist rule in China.

It is being done through the so-called "learning movement". Learning classes are conducted in all schools, factories, government offices and public organisations which have been brought under state control. Communist representatives stationed in these organisations make the encouragement of learning their first duty.

The "learning movement" is designed to make every Chinese a political supporter of the communist regime. It teaches Marxism, Leninism and Mao Tse-tung's theories. Its chief precepts at this initial stage are: (1) Communism is the perfect and only democratic system, and the best solution for all evils; (2) Soviet Russia is China's only true friend and is not an imperialistic power; and (3) the United States is an imperialist power and, therefore, China's enemy.

Another purpose of the "learning movement" is to acquaint the people with, and to convince them of, the wisdom of current communist policies. Even university professors are required to attend the learning classes, although most of them know more about Marxism and Leninism than the communist instructors who teach them. Political indoctrination is the prerequisite to getting a job with the communists.

The communists have achieved solid success in their indoctrination programme. I know of many of my friends who have had their thinking radically changed after a few months in an indoctrination camp. But the programme as a whole has evoked dissatisfaction.

The average Chinese habitually cares little for politics. What he wants most is a peaceful and good livelihood. Most of them were dissatisfied because they were required to spend many hours a week in addition to the normal working hours in tiring, and to them, uninteresting political meetings.

Their dissatisfaction was heightened on many occasions when they found out that they were not only required to attend political meetings, but also to express opinions at the meetings, as silence is interpreted by the communists as a "sign of reactionary passiveness".

Several of them told me, "We don't mind attending the classes because we want to retain our jobs. But what gets us is the requirement that we have to say something in the classes and say only what the communists like to hear".

The educated class has no objections to gaining any new knowledge, but they dislike the communist requirement that not only must they learn, but they must accept what they are taught in the indoctrination classes as their own philosophy of life.

2. Communist Efforts to Disguise Totalitarianism

The Chinese communists are covering up their totalitarian system under a cloak of high-sounding democratic terminology and pretensions.

The communists' arch pretension is that theirs is the only real democracy. They believe that they represent the people and that their party and government are the people's party and the people's government. Therefore, what they say and do and advocate is what the people should say and do and advocate. Otherwise, anyone opposing them is opposing the people, and to say that they do not represent the people or that their system is not democratic is blasphemy and a capital offence.

At present one of the chief missions of their propaganda is to smear the Western political system, which the majority of educated Chinese had accepted as true democracy, as "false democracy". The reason they give is that the Western system is dominated by the capitalist class, which is in the minority, for the purpose of exploiting and oppressing the majority. They call their present transition political set-up in Peking a system of "democratic concentration". The basic principle of the system, according to Premier Chou En-lai, is that the minority shall obey the majority and the lower levels shall obey the higher levels.

In practice these basic principles rarely apply. To mention just one out of the many violations of these principles: the minority opinion (Communist Party) prevailed over the majority opinion (non-party democratic parties and "personages") in the selection of the national flag in the People's Political Consultative Conference in Peking last September. The majority opinion, according to the *Takungpao*, favoured a flag with one five-pointed star on a red background with a nationalistic yellow stripe running across the middle of the flag symbolising the Yellow River, the "Cradle of Chinese Civilisation".

The communists call their permanent system which will follow the present coalition set-up in Peking a "People's Democratic Dictatorship". This, in the minds of many Chinese, is a contradiction in terms. Mao Tse-tung in his treatise on the "People's Democratic Dictatorship" on July 1 explained that it is democratic because political power is vested in the hands of the people and a dictatorship because it denies political power to those who are not the people.

The next question that occurs in the minds of observers is: Who are the people? The communist conception of the "people" is fluid and changes with time. Currently they are the workers, farmers, petty bourgeoisie and the so-called national bourgeois (that is, the money class not connected with bureaucratic capital); or, in short, those who support the communists, even if they are former warlords or feudalistic landlords. The New China News Agency has yet to explain who will constitute the "people" in the future.

Despite communist explanations of their political system, in the opinion of neutral observers, it is a one-party dictatorship similar to the Kuomintang regime. Once this correspondent asked a communist, "How can you call your system democratic when it is actually your party that rules?" His answer was curt: "That shows your thinking has not yet been 'broken open'". ("Broken open" is a new communist term meaning to accept communist dialectics.)

Lower in the administrative levels, the communists also have their "democratic" practices:

Free elections. Admittedly, voters are given full freedom in casting their vote, but all of the candidates are selected by the communists. Sometimes there are oversights on the part of communist supervisors, but they are corrected immediately in a brusque manner. For instance, the Shanghai Arts College was asked to elect several student delegates to a meeting shortly after the "liberation" of the city. The students thought it was a free election and promptly elected their delegates, but soon afterwards the election list of communist-approved candidates arrived. Before the situation could be remedied the elected delegates had already gone to the meeting. There at the gate, however, they were denied admission because their names were not on the list.

Democratic discussion. Again admittedly, discussion is democratic, but all opinions expressed are usually favourable to the communists because the participants are selected. In open meetings, arrangements are made beforehand to ensure a favourable trend in the deliberations. For instance, a meeting of business guilds was called in Nanking last July by the Tax Bureau director to discuss the rate of the business tax for May and June. The amount of the tax for the two months had already been fixed by the director at forty thousand piculs (approximately seventeen piculs to one ton) of rice.

In the meeting, many guild representatives raised objections and demanded a reduction, but they were promptly shouted down by bookstore representatives as "reactionaries". The director made a long speech defending the tax as being in the interest of the people. There was a prolonged silence. The bookstore representatives rose and said that since no further contrary opinions were expressed it showed that the participants had come to a "higher degree of political understanding" and moved that the tax be supported and the meeting closed. The next morning the *New China Daily* reported that after full consultation with guild representatives in a "democratic spirit" the Government received "unanimous and enthusiastic" support for the business tax.

The people's demand. When the communists take a suppressive measure, it is usually preceded by letters to editors in the newspapers' readers' column demanding such a measure. Thus, the foreign press was banned because "the people had demanded it".

Voluntariness. When the communists make the people do something, their tactics are to make them do it "voluntarily". Thus, workers are reported to have "voluntarily" reduced their salary and worked longer hours, coolies "voluntarily" carried loads for the communist army, office employees "voluntarily" resigned to go back to the village to produce, and so forth.

To mention just two out of the many instances of "voluntariness" which have come to my attention:

First, a staff member in the Nanking Irrigation Bureau was discharged in the recent austerity campaign, but was asked by the communist departmental chief to sign a paper saying he had "voluntarily resigned to return to the village to produce". The man refused. He was then subjected to an exhaustive process of "persuasion" by the departmental chief and was called in to the chief's office every hour. After five rounds of "persuasion" he finally submitted.

Second, the students of a girl's middle school in Nanking refused to join the parades in celebration of the establishment of the new people's government. Communist students went in to ask the principal to "persuade" the students to join in the parade "voluntarily". The principal at first declined to do so, but later agreed and called a meeting of the whole student body. The students still refused to join. The principal finally announced that she would join. That broke the stalemate and the students went to the parade "voluntarily".

Hope. When the communists want the people to do something not in the line of duty but which they deem to be politically significant, such as parades, their tactic is to tell them, "We hope you will do it". "Hope" has now come to be understood as an order, because several workers in a factory in Nanking who neglected to join in a recent parade as they were "hoped" to do were discharged for other specious reasons.

3. Democratic Spirit Within the Communist Party

Despite totalitarianism in state rule, the democratic spirit prevails within the Chinese Communist Party.

The Chinese Communist Party, as its counterparts in other countries, is tightly organised, requiring absolute obedience and discipline from its members. But party decision and action are always preceded by democratic discussion. Its democratic spirit is best demonstrated by mutual and self criticism, confession, repentance, and pardon.

In the administrative office the subordinate obeys his superior, but in the "learning" or "work-review" meeting, held virtually every day after or before office hours, rank is ignored. All are comrades on an equal footing, and an orderly is free to criticise his army commander if he likes.

Even Mao Tse-tung, the undisputed leader of the party, is not exempt. Premiere Chou En-lai, in a speech in Peking, revealed that Mao had been severely criticised many times in the old Yenan days.

"Work-review" meetings are said to be an effective weapon in boosting organisational and administrative efficiency and also in boosting fighting morale in the army. Communist sources said that after every battle, meetings are held between officers and men to discuss the strategy followed.

These sources said that many officers were removed because their men complained of bad leadership, and many men were known to have displayed greater valour after they were branded cowards at the meetings. One source said

General Chen Yi, Third Field Army Commander, once shed tears in apology and repentance when his men flayed him with good reason for faulty tactics in a particular action.

The average communist is imbued with a large amount of sporting spirit. He does not feel hurt when criticised by his comrades, nor does he hesitate to criticise himself, confess, and repent when he makes a mistake. In Nanking, the manager of the Communist Trade Bureau flirted with a non-communist girl in his office and used the office jeep too often for private purposes. He was immediately criticised and was dismissed for harbouring petty bourgeoisie thoughts.

Confession is an extenuation, and when made immediately after an offence the offender usually has only to make a public apology. Thus, in Nanking, the newspaper reader comes across daily advertisements of apology inserted by black market dealers and other lawbreakers. Twelve pro-Kuomintang professors of Nanking University (formerly National Central University) were reinstated after they confessed their "reaction" thoughts at a joint meeting of the faculty staff and students.

These democratic practices are, in effect, a process for purging the party of diversionism. They mean inevitably frequent and long meetings. In addition to the normal eight office hours, the average communist member has to put in another three to four hours a day for meetings.

The common daily routine of a communist official is: Up at six a.m.; "learning" meeting at six-thirty a.m.; office, eight a.m. to noon and one to five p.m.; "work-review" meeting seven p.m. sometimes till midnight.

The average communist member, probably because of his political training, is a long-winded speech-maker. A speech always lasts at least two hours and a shorter speech is a rarity. The longest speech known to the public was one made by Premier Chou En-lai at the meeting of the Preparatory Committee of the National Scientists' Association, which ran over seven hours with only a ten minute interval.

The Chinese communists are now faced with a serious shortage of personnel in running the expanding areas under their control. The shortage is aggravated by their reluctance to employ "outsiders" because of their suspicion of non-communists. In the newly-occupied territories, they are solving the problem by making one department do the work of several departments and one man do the work of several men.

The communists have established training camps in practically all the major cities to train non-communists for administrative jobs. The training in these "universities" is essentially political indoctrination, because in the eyes of the communists political qualification ranks above experience, technical skill, and knowledge in public service.

At the present time the communists are drawing upon their manpower resources in the old "liberated" territories to run their expanding domain. In some old liberated areas, their administrative staff has dwindled to only twenty *kanpus* (rank and file) for each *hsien* (county), where formerly there used to be one *kanpu* for every three villages. These village *kanpus* are mostly raw country boys who, though firm and thorough in their devotion to revolutionary ideals, are of a low educational and intellectual level. Some of them, now heading large administrative departments in the newly-occupied areas south of the Yangtse River, cannot even read, just as the judges in the Nanking People's Court cannot.

The *kanpus* are usually restricted in their knowledge of the outside world, presumably because of their "lean to one side" indoctrination. Some communist *kanpus* went to Shanghai with the belief that the atomic bomb does not exist because they were told in the villages by their political commissioners that it was merely imperialist propaganda.

Some of the communists are so over-zealous in their devotion to revolutionary ideals that they sometimes unconsciously encourage lawlessness. This is especially evident in their sponsorship of the cause of the poor. The following instances illustrate this point:

(1) The owner of a timber shop in Nanking one day caught a burglar and took him to the police station.

The next morning a police officer came back with the burglar and asked the owner to employ him, saying, "He steals because he has no money. He has no money because he has no employment. So if you give him a job he won't steal anymore". The owner protested, but the police officer was insistent and the owner was compelled to employ the burglar. Two days later the owner gave the burglar some money and told him to quit.

(2) Last June a crowd of poor men and women forced their way into a construction project to collect pieces of wood and other odds and ends. The gateman was unable to stop them, so he reported the pilferage to a Liberation Army guard. The guard, however, told him to be calm, saying: "You have lots of wood. They are poor people. There's no harm in giving them some of your wood".

4. The Threat of Diversionism Inside the Communist Party

One of the greatest threats during the next few years to the communist programme of creating a totalitarian China may come from within the Communist Party itself.

This threat is diversionism, which has already cropped up among the rank and file of the party and army.

The existence of liberalism, democratic individualism, nationalistic patriotism, and laxity in party and army discipline has been openly admitted by communist newspapers.

"Incorrect" implementation of policies on the part of communist administrative officials and a relaxation in the revolutionary spirit, crystallised in the sentiment of "now that we have got it let's take it easy", have been reported.

In contradistinction to departure from the "party line", there is also what communist leaders describe as "ultra-leftist" tendencies in adhering to the "party line", endangering the many devious measures which the Communist High Command is adopting to achieve totalitarianism.

Especially distasteful to the ultra-leftists are:

(1) The communist policies of "cooperation" with the so-called democratic parties and "personages" in which these parties and "personages" are given a share in the new political power and treated as "royal guests" in Peking; and

(2) The policy of permitting private businesses and industries in the urban areas.

One of the results of these policies is that many communists who went through years of hardship and danger in the revolutionary struggle found themselves being asked to continue to bear hardships and danger, while men who had not made any active contribution towards, or were ideologically against, the revolution are given high official positions and a comfortable livelihood. This gave rise to the popular complaint among the "ultra-leftists" that "to be an old revolutionary is not as good as to be a new revolutionary. And to be a new revolutionary is not as good as a non-revolutionary".

This dislike of the new revolutionaries is evidenced in the action of lower-ranking communist officials adopting a "closed door" policy in the admission of members to the New Democracy Youth Corps which, according to regulations laid down by the Communist High Command, is open to youths of all creeds for indoctrination as potential members of the Communist Party.

The New China News Agency once issued an editorial castigating party members who opposed the policy of permitting private ownership of land and capital in the urban areas. The Agency explained that origin of private ownership of lands and capital in the cities is different from that in the rural districts. In the rural districts, people acquire land and capital without working for the acquisition, while in the cities owners obtain their assets by investment and hard work.

In addition, there are signs of divergent sentiments on several basic political issues. For instance, one communist member told me in a private conversation that new China would fight all imperialists, including Soviet Russia if she is found to be also imperialistic. Such doubt about Soviet Russia is taboo in the eyes of the doctrinaire communists whose conviction is that Soviet Russia cannot be imperialistic.

Another instance is the belief of a high-ranking communist official in Nanking that the anti-United States policy of the new government is merely a "propaganda stunt" and not an unchangeable state policy. In a conversation with a friend of this correspondent, the official advised him to tell his American friends not to worry about the "propaganda stunt".

There are signs of cliques within the party which are more evident in the East China area, where for several months General Chen Yi's Third Field Army and General Liu Po-chen's Second Field Army exercised joint control. There were known cases of wrestling for technical personnel between the two field army commands, and also cases of wrestling for power between Army Commander Chen Yi's men and those under his political commissar, Jao Shu-shih, and between the "technical men" faction and "political men" faction in Shanghai.

There are also the conflicting factions of the old and new *kanpus*. The old *kanpus* are members who had joined the party since the old Kiangsi days. Most of them are veterans of six-thousand-mile Long March from Kiangsi to Yenan in the middle 1930s, but they are mostly of an extremely low educational level. Some of them cannot read or write a letter, but because of their length of service they are appointed heads of departments or bureaus in the expanding communist administrative machine.

The new *kanpus* are generally of a high educational level, being mostly graduates of middle schools or universities. They joined the party much later than the old *kanpus* and are now serving as subordinates of the old *kanpus*. The conflict between these two factions is that the old *kanpus* are jealous of their better-educated subordinates and the new *kanpus* are disgruntled because they have to serve under less-educated men. The conflict is most evident in the interior districts.

The Communist Party, according to the New China News Agency, now has a membership of over three million. If this is true, it would mean that the Party has grown very rapidly since the end of World War II because in 1945 Premier Chou En-lai announced in Chungking that the Party's membership was between 900,000 and one million. Observers believe that during the process of this rapid growth, many insufficiently-indoctrinated men and women of faltering loyalty must have been taken in, despite the rigid admission regulations.

Communist admission regulations contain different provisions for non-intellectuals and intellectuals. Non-intellectuals, such as illiterate farmers and workers, may be given full membership after three months' probation. For intellectuals, or the "shaky" elements as many communists call them and of whom the communists are habitually suspicious, the probation period may take anywhere from one to five years. For students the communists make a special concession, probably because of their active support in the overthrow of the Kuomintang. They may be taken into the Party after a minimum period of six months' probation.

There is also evidence that within the rank and file of the Communist Party the human element has already started to make itself felt vis-à-vis the communist ideological disregard for human nature.

I was told in Nanchang that there is some dissidence among communist members against the Party's regulations governing marriage. These regulations provide that a communist shall marry a communist, the marriage must receive the prior approval of the superior authorities and the prospective bride's thought must be investigated. The ration between women and men in the Communist Party is one to between fifty and one hundred. As most of the female members go for the higher-ups, the average communist male cannot find a wife.

Diversionism is still confined to the minority of the communist rank and file, but it is spreading and apparently is regarded with concern by the Communist High Command. Many communist commanders, including Mao Tse-tung, Liu Po-chen and Lin Piao, on several occasions publicly reprimanded the diversionists.

In Nanking, a party meeting was held last September to conduct a "purge of thought" and strengthen organisational discipline.

The majority of communist members are, it is generally conceded by neutral observers, still conscientious and loyal revolutionaries. There is universal praise for their devotion to their revolutionary cause and ideals and their spirit of self-denial and self-sacrifice. Their capacity for "eating hardships" is also considered exemplary. The average communist *kanpu* works ten to fourteen hours a day. He is given lodging, food and clothing of the lowest grade and is paid the equivalent of two packets of native cigarettes a month for pocket money. If he is married, his wife must work to support herself.

The strain of overwork and poor living conditions over a number of years has had telling effects on the health of the communists. According to one Nanking doctor who was given a temporary appointment in the medical corps, tuberculosis, neurosis and night blindness – all due to under-nourishment and over-exertion – are the most common diseases in the Liberation Army. For the purpose of maintaining the spiritual morale of individual workers, tuberculosis is recorded as bronchitis in one communist organisation in Nanking.

5. Communist "Lean to One Side" Principle

The chief political principle of the Chinese communists is "lean to one side".

Mao Tse-tung made a powerful exposition of the principle in his famous July 1st speech on the "People's Democratic Dictatorship". He said, "In order to win and consolidate victory, we must lean to one side... To sit on the fence is impossible; a third road does not exist... Neutrality is a camouflage".

This principle applies to all communist policies and actions and governs individual conduct and thinking. It is designed to bring about a oneness in all spheres of action – one kind of thought, one kind of education, one kind of news, one kind of truth, one kind of literature, and so forth. And always the communist kind.

Applied to the individual, it means he must believe in and accept communist theories and rules of conduct. He must not be an anti-communist or "reactionary" in the communist language, and he must also not be an independent or neutral. It is described as the tightest restriction on civil liberty and a heavy blow to the democratic individuals or free-thinkers who constitute the majority of the Chinese population.

In foreign policy, it requires unconditional alignment with Soviet Russia and the Soviet satellites. This is where the application of the principle has aroused much scepticism among the politically-minded Chinese, who maintain that neutrality in international politics and a friendship with the West would help much more than unconditional alignment with Soviet Russia in the task of rehabilitating war-wrecked China.

Many attempts have been made to persuade the communists to abandon their "lean to one side" principle at least in foreign policy, but to no avail. Hsiao Chun, the well-known Chinese Leftist writer who had been a communist supporter since he began his public career, made the first attempt. Beginning in August 1948, he wrote a series of articles in his journal *Culture* in Harbin, criticising the "lean to one side" principle. He noted that Soviet Russia is also imperialistic and that to make Marxism, Leninism and Mao Tse-tung's theories the only education for the Chinese people would be a "one-colour purge" or "mechanical unity". Hsiao was immediately dubbed a reactionary and diversionist, despite his long record of loyal service to the communists, and exiled to a factory "to learn from the workers whom he had insulted".

A qualified source said "a very high personage" had recently talked to Mao Tse-tung for four hours trying to obtain a modification of the "lean to one side" principle. The source refused to reveal the identity of the "very high personage", but said that he is not the first one to talk to Mao on the subject.

In the People's Political Consultation Conference held in Peking in September 1949, the "democratic personages" had also raised, according to a communist source in Shanghai, suggestions for a modification of the principle in the fields of foreign and internal policy, and the discussion at one stage became so heated that Mao Tse-tung was obliged to intervene with a firm declaration that "we must and will lean to one side".

Communist explanations to non-communist opponents of the principle is this: We have not yet stood on our feet and we cannot for the present afford to show the slightest lack of friendship for Soviet Russia, which has a long common borderline with our country. In the future, after we have put our house in order, we may reconsider the whole problem.

Current communist totalitarian policies, such as regimentation of social life, political indoctrination and control of the press, are designed to implement this principle.

The thorough realisation of the principle, in the eyes of the communists, is the key to making communism a political success in China, although it is feared among many political circles that its implementation may cause the contrary result because of its obvious unsuitability to Chinese conditions.

Special emphasis is being laid on the principle in indoctrination classes. The communist representative in the Shanghai China Textiles Incorporated told the workers one day that there are "only three roads open to you: either lean to our side or go abroad to become a 'White Chinese' or commit suicide". It is common to hear communist officials declaring in public speeches that "either you are for us or against us, either a progressive or a reactionary. There is no middle road".

The communist policies for one-colour ideological purge and their intolerance of opposition are based on:

First, their belief in the perfection of their political system and that their system is the only real democratic one in the world, which brings them to the conclusion that all the other systems must be scrapped as historical junk.

Second, their system cannot thrive as long as other kinds of systems exist.

These two communist concepts run counter to the widely-accepted law of evolution that everything is dynamic, not static, and everything develops and improves and nothing is perfect.

They are also contrary to the precept of the Western democracies that the existence of opposition is not necessarily a death warrant for a political system. It actually is a most vital factor in true democracy. Whether a political system can continue to exist depends more on its intrinsic conformity with the interests of the people and the state rather than on the existence of opposition. If a system really receives the majority support of the common man, it will stay regardless of how serious the political opposition is. If not, it will be overthrown by the political opposition. In such cases, democratic statesmanship requires acceptance of defeat in a sportive spirit.

The best illustration of the communist belief in the aforementioned communist concepts is a talk between Mao Tse-tung and a prominent Chinese professor of law, who had since joined the communists. This professor, disgusted with the Kuomintang, journeyed to Yenan towards the end of the Sino-Japanese War. In his first talk with Mao Tse-tung, he asked the communist leader why there was all this violent anti-American propaganda and attitude. Mao replied that they had to do it, because it is a question of "whether we survive or they survive. The two cannot live under the same sky".

Another difference in ideology between the communists and the Western democracies is that the communists believe that economic socialism can only be carried out under a system of totalitarianism, whereas the West believes that it can be carried out under a system of political democracy. The Father of the Chinese Republic, Dr. Sun Yat-sen, subscribed to the belief of the Western democracies. This is generally presumed to be the main reason why the communists banned the teaching of his Three People's Principles in the schools.

Many Chinese youths whom I talked to toe the communist line because they believe that the main political trend throughout the world nowadays is towards economic socialism and that the people will have to throw in their lot with the communists sooner or later. If this is so, they reason, it is better to throw in their lot with the communists now rather than later. These youths are correct in their belief that the world is heading towards socialism, but they seem to have overlooked the fact that there are two kinds of socialism: one under a system of totalitarianism, such as the one in Soviet Russia, and one under a system of political democracy, such as the one in Britain.

The communist "lean to one side" principle was the cause of a dramatic incident in Nanking in August 1949. At the conclusion of a two-month indoctrination course for middle and primary school teachers, the communist educational representative Chao Cho told the teachers that they henceforth must "lean to one side". An aged teacher stood up and said, "Yes, we are going to lean to one side. During the Yuan Shih-kai days, I leaned to his side and what he said and did was wisdom to me. After the Peking warlords were ousted by the Kuomintang, I leaned to the other side of the Kuomintang and what they said and did was wisdom to me. Then came the Japanese and Wang Ching-wei. Each time I leaned to one side, too. After V-J Day, I leaned back to the side of the Kuomintang. Now you have come. I will without doubt lean to your side". The aged teacher's speech sent Chao into a rage. Chao shouted, "That's opportunism, not the kind of learning we want!" The aged teacher quietly retorted, "Mr. Chao, there's nothing else I can do. I have to live".

6. The Merits and Demerits of the Communist Government

Last August, Chinese communist leader Mao Tse-tung showed a long letter to the first conference of the representatives of all classes convened in Peking to review the city government's administrative policies. It had been written to him by an anonymous citizen, who had drawn an eye on the envelope. Mao did not give his interpretation of the meaning of the eye, but presumable the writer was appealing to the communist leader to open his eyes to see things happening outside his closely guarded house.

The writer complained of economic inflation, price fluctuations, frequent readjustment of public utility rates, impoverished livelihood, business and industrial stagnation, increasing unemployment and heavy taxes, levies and assessments, yet he praised the forbearing spirit of the communist workers and the Army's good discipline.

Mao did not reveal the remaining contents of the letter. He said that the writer's opinion was that the communists are "better, but not much better" than the Kuomintang. Mao commented, "This opinion is just".

Mao said that the writer wanted him to give a public reply in the *People's Daily*. He said he would rather leave it to the conference to reply to the writer's complaints. The conference altered its agenda and devoted the rest of the meeting to a discussion of the contents of the letter. The following is a resume of the discussion as reported by the *Takungpao*:

One delegate said that the communists were not responsible for the present difficulties, which he alleged were the outcome of the Kuomintang misrule and disruption by Kuomintang underground agents. He said the communists were presently doing their utmost to rectify these "abnormal conditions" with special emphasis on the improvement of the people's livelihood and encouraging the unemployed to return to the villages to produce. Mr. Peng Chen, the communist chairman of the conference, acknowledged the existence of the difficulties of which the anonymous citizen had complained, but said they were the "concomitants of victory".

He said, "The current price fluctuations are due to speculation and hoarding by traitorous merchants and the influx of capital from Shanghai, though our own imperfect economic controls are also to blame.... The people's livelihood admittedly has still not been improved and the taxes, levies and assessments are still heavy, but the solution to these problems must await the complete liberation of the entire country, which will permit the diversion of the great power of the Liberation Army to production". Chairman Peng's analysis was unanimously adopted as the reply to the anonymous complainant.

The anonymous citizen's complaints are well representative of the majority opinion among the Chinese population: the communist government is definitely better than the outgoing Kuomintang regime in administration, and many people maintain that it would be deplorable if they fail.

The communists' good points are their comparative thoroughness, cleanliness and efficiency of administration, the discipline of the Army, the conscientious, patriotic and forbearing spirit of their workers and their elimination of the many evil, feudalistic and obsolete customs and institutions.

Their weaknesses are considered to be their lack of real democracy, their "lean to one side" foreign policy, their political radicalism and their lack of administrative personnel and knowledge.

It is the consensus among political observers that the communist government minus its totalitarianism and "lean to one side" foreign policy would be the best for China and communist workers, minus their political bias, would be the ideal administrator for the country.

The lower-ranking and especially rural communist *kanpus* are the most obsessed with the political bias. Unlike their top leaders in Peking and other major cities, they rarely show consideration for public feelings. This makes them act exactly according to the "Party Line" and thus appear devoid of feeling to the common man.

At present, it is only in the rural districts, interior cities and small townlets that the real face of communism has unfolded. Real communism has yet to come to the main cities, notably Shanghai. Shanghai is considered the most fortunate city in communist China, because civil liberties exist on much the same scale as before. For instance, professors in Shanghai, unlike their colleagues in other cities, have not been required to undergo a period of political indoctrination. In rural districts, people putting on a good dress or buying a chicken for dinner or conversing in a group of more than five people frequently get into hot waters.

Higher-ranking communists are also considered much better than the lower-ranking *kanpus*. One common comment among Chinese circles is that the high-ranking *kanpus* are too good, the middle-ranking *kanpus* too few, and the lower-ranking *kanpus* too inconsiderate.

Many Shanghai industrialists and commercial leaders who were disgusted with local communist authorities were known to have brightened in outlook after a visit to the top communist leaders in Peking, whom they found to be sympathetic to their opinion and troubles. Some of them brought their problems to the top communist leaders after they had failed to affect a settlement with the local *kanpus*. Shanghai industrialist Chien Chia-hsun illustrated the following story in a public speech showing how top communists had intervened to remedy "misgovernment" by local *kanpus*:

The Tientsin Chihhsin Cement Company made a contract with the communist Trade Bureau for the sale of all its cement production to the Bureau for a period of eight months. The price was fixed at RMB$4,000 per bag, which was a good price at the time of the signing of the contract. However, due to inflation the price became unrealistic and the company incurred heavy losses. The communist Trade Bureau refused to readjust the price.

The Tientsin Chiuta Salt Company during the first few months of communist occupation found no market for its salt. All the markets were monopolised by the Communist Trade Bureau. The company sent a consignment of salt to Lingching for sale. When its salt arrived there, the local communist bureau forced down prices and the company incurred heavy losses.

The two companies appealed to Liu Shao-chi, No. 2 Communist (the leader next to Mao Tse-tung), who journeyed to Tientsin and investigated the matter. He immediately ordered a new cement contract with a flexible price and ordered the Communist Trade Bureau in Lingching to cease its "forcing-down-price" policy.

Despite the good showing of the communists in administration and army discipline, many observers feel uncertain regarding the future. The popular question is: Will they be good forever or will they deteriorate in the course of time as the Kuomintang did, which also had shown high standards in government and army discipline at the beginning?

I have come across many evidences of administrative malpractice in army discipline similar to those prevalent within the Kuomintang. Corruption has been reported by the communist papers. Army commanders Lin Piao and Liu Po-chen have on several occasions reprimanded their men publicly for malpractices.

My experience is that the communists behave with greater correctitude in the cities than in the rural districts, and more in the beginning than as time goes by. Bullying of the *laopaihsing* (common people) and the forceful occupation of private property by army men and misappropriation of public materials by administrative officials in the small townlets and villages are frequently reported by the communist papers. As far as I know, these malpractices very rarely happen in the cities.

In Shanghai, the communist army showed exemplary discipline at the beginning, but a few months later deterioration crept in. Once I saw a communist soldier driving away pedicabs and coolies with a long pole, which was the bullying method used by Kuomintang troops and which no one would expect the well-disciplined communist soldiers to be capable of.

These malpractices are still in the insignificant stage. The communist problem is how to contain them from spreading in a system which bans the existence of a critically informed public opinion and popularly-elected assemblies.

7. Disillusionment and Discontent in Communist China

Many people in communist China feel that a third world war would be preferable to living under the communists. There is widespread disillusionment and discontent with communist rule in China, mainly because of the impoverished living conditions. There is a general desire for something new and better than the communist government. Most of the disillusioned and discontented people see a third world war as the only solution for their troubles. Some even wish for the return of the Kuomintang.

The New China News Agency reported that rebelling peasants in some areas, such as Manchuria, are also banking on the possibility of a third world war and are using it as one of their chief political slogans.

Although anti-communist feelings are reportedly more widespread in the rural areas and small towns than in the major cities where the communists are more lenient and less radical in their policies, resentment is still evident in the major cities. In Nanking seven out of ten people I talked to expressed anti-communist views for one reason or another with five of the seven showing an interest in another global flare-up.

Disillusionment and discontent is now held down by the military might of the communist army and police, but in some rural areas where communist political power has not been firmly established it has erupted into armed opposition. These areas include Manchuria, Honan, Anhwei, Kiangsi, and Shantung provinces. The backbone of the residence movement is reportedly composed mainly of Chinese secret village societies, such as the Red Spear Society, which were formed hundreds of years ago originally for the purpose of self protection and opposing Manchuria rule.

The New China News Agency reported in July 1949 that practically all the village societies in Honan province, about 165 in number, were in revolt against the communists.

The best organised resistance group is said to be the Ninth Route Army now based in the Tapiehshan Mountains in the Honan-Anhwei-Hupeh border region, which only one year ago was the chief operation base of the famous one-eyed communist General Liu Po-chen.

The Ninth Route Army, namely apparently in contradistinction to the Communist Eighth Route Army, is in control of large areas in the Central China provinces, as indicated by a New China News Agency report that communist suppression forces after two months had succeeded in ousting it from two districts in Anhwei containing a population of over four million men. The Ninth Route Army is said to have a political programme the aims of which are indicated by its slogans "Down with Chiang Kai-shek" and "Capture Mao Tse-tung alive".

Many of the rebelling peasants appear to have united themselves into a secret organisation called the *Yikuantao* (the Society of the Consistent Way). Communist reports talked of revolting *Yikuantao* peasants north of the Yangtse River, extending even as north as Manchuria. In Manchuria, communist reports charged that the rebellion was instigated by the Buddhist monks and nuns and by the underground agents of the Kuomintang and American "imperialism".

Despite the widespread nature of the peasant uprisings, competent observers doubt they will be effective enough to prevent the communists from consolidating their rule, because the rebellious peasantry is unorganised and has no political leadership or political cause to sustain them in their struggle. They are fighting the communists mainly because of the crippling taxes, levies and assessments. In some areas in Honan, there was recently a decrease in uprisings after the communists reduced the various imposts on the people.

Discontent in the major cities is beginning to be expressed openly. Anti-communist posters have appeared in some cities and verses were coined in scorn of the communists. Three of the more popular verses are:

(1) *The communists are good, but we have not enough to eat; Chiang Kai-shek is bad, but we have a bellyful.*

(2) *The communists have liberated us, but our counters are growing moss.* (This is sung by businessmen in reference to the economic depression.)

(3) *We have turned over our body, but it is like turning over form the bed to the ground.* (Turning over the body in Chinese is *fansheng*, which means emancipation from slavery or political oppression. This is sung by the labouring class.)

Another current open expression of anti-communist feelings in the urban areas is the rewording of communist political songs. The second sentence of one song which reads, "Out of China comes a Mao Tse-tung" became

"Out of China comes a Mao Tsa-chung". *Tsachung* is a contemptuous term meaning "mongrel breed". The first sentence of another song reads, "The skies of the liberated areas are downcast skies". On several occasions I heard the reworded songs sung in Nanking streets, when there were no communist soldiers or officials around.

Despite the widespread disillusionment, some people tried to toe the communist line just for the sake of earning a livelihood. Because of the rigid communist dictatorship, the communist line is very narrow and many of those who tried to toe the line found it difficult to do. When the communists established their first indoctrination "university" in Nanking, over ten thousand young men enrolled, hoping that after a few months training they would be given jobs. Before the second month was over, about half of them had taken French leave.

One prominent woman leader in Shanghai got along with the communists very smoothly for several months until a slip of the tongue in a public meeting. In the meeting she, being a "democratic personage", was called upon to make a speech. The main theme of her speech in referring to current national affairs was: *Before we had no ship. Now we have a ship but no rudder.* In other words, the political is important, but it requires the coordination of the technical. Communist listeners interpreted her words as meaning that in her opinion the technical is more important than the political, which is contrary to communist ideology. The next day a petition was presented to the Shanghai Democratic Women's Union for her resignation.

As the situation stands now, most of the people under the communists are living in a state of nervous tension. They are uncertain of tomorrow, as anything may happen. The farmers fear more and heavier levies; the workers, longer working hours, reduction of salary or even dismissal; and the businessmen, more and heavier taxes. The schoolteachers and university professors fear that they may be transferred to more laborious jobs or say something wrong in class causing them to lose their employment.

Most of the intellectual class are now in a state of *koonmen* (gloomy sadness). *Koonmen* is a term now popularly used in China to designate disillusionment and dissatisfaction with communist rule.

The communists display a sharp dislike and suspicion of intellectuals, whom they call the "shaky" element, presumably because they are more inclined to ask questions than the uneducated people.

Most of the university professors are now locking themselves in their houses, reading books and going out very little, except to classes. These people had been most active in the former agitation against the Kuomintang one-party rule, but they have come to realise that the present changeover is bringing them no brighter hope for the democracy for which they had been yearning for the last few decades.

Koonmen sentiments have also arisen among the students, who were considered the strongest supporters of the communists during the Kuomintang days. In Shanghai, where communist political power has yet to be firmly established in the minds of the people, there are already signs of organised student opposition against the communists.

A high communist educational official, admitting there are "signs" of opposition, confided that the Red regime would take drastic action if this continued. Opposition is strongest in the private Ta-Hsia (Great China) University and the American-endowed University of Shanghai. This is presently crystallising into a battle for the control of student organisations. The Ta-Hsia anti-Red students, who call themselves middle-roaders, succeeded in ousting the Reds from the control of forty percent of the university's department student societies.

Opposition is also strong in private secondary schools in Shanghai. Pro-Red and anti-Red students in the assembly hall segregate themselves into two groups, one singing the new Red anthem, the other the nationalist anthem. The communist authorities are presently adopting a tolerant attitude towards these recalcitrants, but several anti-Red student leaders have been arrested for "mistaken thoughts". Teenage secondary school students are also exhibiting disgust of the new regime by asking all kinds of embarrassing questions in class about Soviet Russia and Soviet control of the Changchun railway, Dairen and Port Arthur.

Students of the Fu-Shin secondary school once proved so difficult that their headmaster was compelled to warn them "to behave or be subject to individual education" (that is, spend time in an indoctrination camp).

Student opposition came into the open during the election of representatives to a student rally held in Shanghai in November 1949. Students of both Ta-Hsia University and the University of Shanghai elected anti-Reds, but the Ta-Hsia Reds immediately annulled the election on the grounds that it was held "without adequate preparation".

The students later found this meant that the list of candidates had not been submitted to the Red-controlled Student City Union for approval. Protests were of no avail, and the Union ordered a new election wherein all candidates were previously screened. The students of one middle school, asked to elect four representatives to a November rally, wrote the names of Lenin, Stalin, Mao Tse-tung, and Chu Teh on the ballots.

The president of the Red-controlled student union, Chang Yu-min, was frequently hissed and booed when lecturing the students on the necessity of submitting to Red rule. Many Nanking students also changed their minds about the Reds. Some asked foreign diplomats to help them arrange passage to Hong Kong and Formosa.

Students in state-owned universities are the most disillusioned group. They had formerly been paid tuition, board and lodging by the Nationalist Ministry of Education, who thus hoped to stem off communist influence among the revolutionary-minded Chinese student class. Following "liberation", the new authorities advised the students that only a few scholarships would be provided for exceptionally bright students. The rest could either continue their education by paying full tuition, or were welcome to join the communist army. Owing to their financial plight, many students were forced to take the latter step.

8. Causes of Disillusionment and Discontent

The disillusioned and discontented people of communist China have a variety of reasons for being so, but the chief reason is that the communists expect too much from them.

Economically, they call upon the individual to work harder and live harder. Politically, they want him to give up his own thinking and follow the communists; that is, do and say what the communists tell him to.

Generally speaking, the individual as the situation stands today has yet to reach the stage of being merely a cog in a machine, but the trend is in that direction. A popular comment is that the communists want the individual to act as docile as a pet dog, work like a bull uncomplainingly, and be loyal to the master at all times.

Psychologically, communist propaganda with its "rosy" promises is chiefly to blame for the widespread dissatisfaction. One of the promises of communist propaganda is that dawn will come to a place upon "liberation", but the fact in all known cases is the contrary and the people's sufferings were deepened subsequent to the changeover. This accounts for the common phenomenon in communist China that before a place is "liberated" the people of the place clamour for communist occupation, but after the people have been subjected to it for several months they change their mind about the communists.

The lack of real freedom and democracy is a matter of general comment. It is the consensus among neutral Chinese quarters that democracy under the communists exists only in name. This creates disillusionment among politically-minded Chinese intellectuals who had formerly thrown in their sympathies with the communists against the Kuomintang in the belief that the communists would at least be more democratic than the Kuomintang.

Communist insistence that their system is the only really democratic one in the world in spite of the facts serves only to embitter popular feelings against them. Communist belief in their ideological infallibility and perfection also is a matter of critical comment.

This belief underlines their intolerance of outside criticism and opposition. Their reasoning is that since they are infallible and perfect there can be nothing wrong with them and any criticism against time is due to malice or cynicism. This presumably is the kind of logic which impelled the communist representative of the Nanking Water Supply Bureau to tell the workers that anyone who opposed his opinion or order was a reactionary.

This dogmatic belief, running counter to the traditional Chinese concept of modesty, has sometimes served to make enemies out of friends. According to education quarters, some students in Shanghai and Nanking became disillusioned with the communists because of this. The students, the quarters said, maintained originally that the communists are much better than the Kuomintang and, therefore, supported them. But the students with their youthful objectiveness also saw some weaknesses in the communist system, and when the communists insisted they were all good it evoked very unfavourable reactions.

Other causes for popular complaint are: (1) communist unconditional alignment with Soviet Russia ideology and foreign policy to the point of "slavishness"; (2) communist anti-American propaganda which is resented by many Western-minded Chinese; and (3) the communist requirement that everyone learn and accept Marxism, Leninism, and Mao Tse-tung's theories as their one and only political belief and philosophy of life.

The political bias of the ordinary communist worker also is another cause of disappointment among the people. That bias makes him appear unreasonable in accordance with traditional Chinese moral concepts in the handling of many public problems. For instance, the communists, prior to discharging a number of employees in the Shanghai Municipal Government in the recent austerity drive, subjected these workers to a two-month period of political indoctrination. At the conclusion of the period, the employees were asked to sign a paper saying they had voluntarily resigned and then been paid off. This appeared unreasonable to the employees. Their complaint was, Why should you put us through a strenuous indoctrination course when you have already decided to terminate our service, and why should we be put on record as having resigned voluntarily when actually we were discharged?

The anti-communist feelings among the common man can best be illustrated by the following two incidents:

First, one night my wife and I were returning home in a pedicab which had no light. I pointed out to the pedicab driver that he was violating traffic regulations. The driver replied, "Violate! Violate! So what! Arrest me! So much the better, because then I would at least have somewhere to sleep and something to eat".

Second, a man consulted a doctor in Nanking. He paid the doctor one silver dollar for the consultation fee. The doctor refused to accept it, because the circulation of silver dollars had been banned by the communists. The doctor suggested he turn it in to the People's Bank as the law requires. The man replied, "If you don't take it, I would rather throw it into the water than give it to the communists".

9. Disillusionment and Discontent Among Workers

Of special political significance is the disillusionment and discontent among the working and farming class.

According to communist ideology, workers and farmers are now the *chu jen ong* (masters or owners) of new China. The Communist Party is a party of workers and farmers. It was for the purpose of liberating them from capitalistic exploitation and bourgeoisie political oppression that the Party was formed.

On the basis of this, workers and farmers should be the first and warmest among communist supporters.

However, the situation in China today is much the reverse. Workers and farmers are the loudest and most active in their complaints against the communists. Most of the anti-communist verses, such as "Chiang Kai-shek is bad, but we eat rice; Mao Tse-tung is good, but we eat millet" and "we have turned over our body [emancipation from political oppression and exploitation] but it's turning over from the bed down to the ground" were coined by workers.

Discontent among workers is easily understandable. After the communists took over, they were required to work longer hours, averaging ten hours a day; in addition, they had to spend approximately four hours a week in political indoctrination classes. They were paid about twenty percent less than before and sometimes required to "voluntarily" further reduce their decreased salaries. They were not allowed to strike or voice their grievances in any other way if the grievances did not conform to communist political ideology.

The right to strike, which workers in Western countries regard as their sacred right, was the subject of a heated debate in the People's Political Consultation Conference last year. Some delegates demanded that the right should be written into the Common Administrative Programme; since private capitalism is permitted during the "New Democracy" period there would be exploitation and the workers should be given the right to strike. But as it was contrary to communist ideology, the demand was squashed.

The ideological communist explanation to the workers is: You are the "masters" of new China and the "owners" of the factory. If you strike, you are striking against yourself. Since the factory is yours, you should work harder and make no fuss about getting lower wages, because it is all your money.

This explanation, however, does not appear to hold much water with the workers. Clashes between workers and communist army guards and of workers deliberately damaging machinery have been reported. Anti-communist posters and poems chalked on walls are common in the workshops. In some factories, workers have even aided Kuomintang underground agents in sabotage, as exemplified in the destruction of several powerful generators in the Shihchingshan power station outside Peking.

Last spring when the workers in the state-owned China Textiles Incorporated factory in Tientsin were agitating for higher wages they were promptly suppressed by a stern warning from the communist representative. The representative reportedly harangued the workers thus: The factory belongs to the government. The government is the people's government. You are the people. Therefore, the factory belongs to you. If you take more money from the factory, you are taking more money from yourselves. Who were the ringleaders? They have misled you. Drive them out.

Working conditions in privately owned factories generally are much better. Communist attempts to extend their control over privately owned factories are often actively resisted by the workers. According to the New China News Agency, the communist representative in a factory in Peking was driven out by the workers. The Agency used this incident as a warning to other communist factory representatives to be more tactful in dealing with the workers.

In Nanking the communists organised a foreigners' house and servants' labour union to help the servants get higher wages and severance pay from their foreign employers. Union officials paid frequent visits to the houseboys, asking them whether they were given the same food as their masters, whether their masters shared their coffee with them and whether they were maltreated in any way.

On one occasion, one foreigner was leaving China. A Union official visited his servants, who told him to quit, saying, "You don't have to come in. We will handle our own affairs. You won't be long here. The Americans and British will come back one day and we will still work for them".

Labour disputes are one of the thorniest problems facing the communists. When it is a dispute between foreigners and Chinese workers, the solution is simple: side with the workers. When it is between state-owned factory and workers, the solution is also simply to tell the workers to shut up. But when it is between privately owned factories and workers, the problem is more complicated.

The workers' demands are usually excessive and the factories usually are in a stagnant state. If the communists favour the workers in accordance with their ideology, the factories would be forced to liquidate, which the communists do not want to see. If they help the management, it will offend the workers, which they also do not want to do. It is like being caught between two fires.

The Shanghai United Press Bureau's labour dispute is one of the best illustrations of how the communists side with the workers against foreign firms. After the communists came into Shanghai, our Bureau found it no longer possible to maintain the news distribution department, because all the newspapers were ordered to use only the service of the New China News Agency. This immediately brought up the problem of terminating all eighteen of the messengers and our workers in the radio room.

Though I had nothing to do with the Shanghai Bureau, my Shanghai colleague (an American) turned over the task of negotiating with the workers on severance pay to me, because of the language facility. I made an agreement on

June 1, 1949, on the workers' own terms for the discharge of nine workers, giving them the equivalent of three to four months' salary in severance pay. I also obtained the verbal agreement of the remaining nine workers that if they were discharged they would be given the same severance pay.

At the beginning of July, we decided to discharge the remaining nine workers. The workers went back on their verbal agreement and asked for three years of termination pay. They might have had a reason for asking for more, perhaps because of the rise of the cost of rice during the interim period. We offered to pay a little more to compensate for the increase, but they insisted on far more than what would constitute a reasonable compensation for the increase of the cost of rice.

I argued and bargained with them for two weeks, but without success. Finally, we brought the dispute before the Communist Labour Union for mediation. When we were all assembled in the Union office with the Union-appointed mediator, the mediator told me to leave the office so that he could hear the views of the workers first. I was called back into the office after half an hour. The union representative, without asking for my arguments, told me that he considered the workers' demands reasonable and suggested I pay them. I protested, point out that it was not acceptable for a mediator to pronounce judgment after having listened only to one side.

After some verbal exchanges, the representative agreed to listen to my arguments. I gave my opinions; he showed a little sympathy for them and asked the workers to consider my offer. The workers, after a short discussion among themselves, refused to accept my offer. We started bargaining again. As the workers frequently changed their demands, I asked that they put their demands in writing as a basis for negotiations. When the workers wrote down their demands, the demands showed another twenty percent increase over what they had originally told the mediator. To my complete surprise, the mediator again deemed their demands "reasonable" and suggested that I pay them. I decided that this was unfair mediation and we left the Union office without any settlement.

After a few more days of fruitless negotiations, the workers pasted anti-American posters all over our office and in the Nanking street outside. We decided then to approach the Communist Foreign Affairs Bureau for mediation. But the Bureau's decision was: Go back to the Labour Union for another mediation. Thereafter, we gave up hope of getting a fair deal from the communists. Finally, I was fortunate enough to prevail upon the workers to trim their demands to six months. But there was a hitch: the workers raised a new demand that I give them a written pledge of priority of employment if the United Press were to reopen in China in the future. This was a shock, but not a problem to me. I willingly gave the pledge, knowing that the United Press would not be able to reopen in China again in the future. But if it does, there should be no problem in re-employing its former workers.

The Communist High Command's directive to their *kanpus* regarding the handling of cases involving private enterprises, according to the New China News Agency is: Act with extreme caution and tact, and maintain strict neutrality, but do the utmost in cutting the demands of workers and inducing management to pay as much as possible. This directive is based on their official economic policy of "benefits to both labour and management".

In actual practice, communist representatives side more with management than with labour, which is another cause of disillusionment among the labouring class. For instance, when the communists entered Wusih in April 1949, the workers in the large Sungsung cotton mills raised several demands which were immediately accepted by the management. The factory was threatened with bankruptcy. Jao Shu-shi, Chief Political Commissioner of the Third Field Army, who was at that time in Tanyang, was informed of the case. He rushed down by special train and called the workers to a meeting. He sternly told them to drop the demands, though they had been already accepted by the management.

Communist representatives sometimes side with labour. This is especially true regarding factories which the communists consider non-essential. The owner of a dye factory in Shanghai committed suicide because he was unable to meet the increased wages approved by the communist labour board. When his partner heard about the suicide, he, too, tried to take his own life by ingesting Lysol, but he was brought back to life by prompt medical treatment. When the workers heard of the tragedy, they waived their demands.

Sometimes the communists leave labour and management to wrangle among themselves, refusing all appeals for mediation. One communist official said he was once called in to mediate a wage dispute in a handkerchief factory. The factory had already suspended operation for some time because of the economic depression which followed communist occupation of the city. The workers demanded ten silver dollars each of living expenses. The owner refused to pay them silver dollars, but was willing to give the workers the equivalent in handkerchiefs because they said that even if they were able to sell them it would be only at a reduced price. Although the communist said he heard arguments from both side and found both sides were reasonable, he still told them to settle the dispute themselves.

10. Disillusion and Discontent Among Farmers

The changeover from nationalism to communism has done nothing to relieve the burden of the Chinese farmers, who are still carrying the heaviest load of any class in China. They are bearing the brunt of financing the war of "liberation", the vast communist army of four to five million men, the government and also the revival of industries. Soviet machinery now being supplied to Manchuria is bartered for food requisitioned from the Manchurian farmers.

According to Kao Kang, chairman of the Manchurian people's government, over four million tons of food were "contributed" by the farmers to the government during the last three years. One third of this was used to buy industrial equipment, Kao said.

According to the communist Finance Minster Ho I-po, the farmers will be called upon to continue to bear the major share of financing the government. In his budget speech on December 2, 1949, he said that "public food" – food requisitioned from the peasants – would be the largest item on the revenue side in 1950, occupying 41.4 percent of the total budgetary income.

The communists, who had been attacking the Kuomintang's food requisition policy, are imposing far heavier food levies on the farmers. The levies are made in the name of requisitions, contributions and supply assessments. Even seeds, straw and firewood are requisitioned.

The levies are imposed on big and small landowners, as well as tenant farmers. The tenants pay seventy percent of the levies. Many farmers in the Nanking-Shanghai area offered to give their land to the communists in lieu of levies and taxes, but the offer was rejected. Some farmers are compelled to sell their furniture and other kinds of movable property to meet the levies.

In some areas the communists allowed months of grace to defaulting farmers until the next harvest for paying the requisitions. In some places, farmers were able to obtain remissions by pleading poverty. Elsewhere the communist *kanpus* were more severe, especially in the villages around Hangchow, where some farmers were reported to have been made to stand in the hot sun the whole day as punishment for their inability to pay the levies. In addition to the levies and taxes, the rural people are subject to radical communist rule by the "old line" unscrupulous *kanpus*. This has resulted in widespread discontent in the rural districts.

Some farmers have been driven to desperation killed communist levy collectors. In other areas farmers left their farms and fled to the cities. A small minority in northern Kiangsu refused to cultivate their lands. Others in southern Shantung cultivated their lands but deliberately refrained from fertilising them. In some districts in the Nanking-Shanghai area, farmers protested by refusing to accept communist currency. In the Kaochiao district southeast of Shanghai, farmers declined to respond to the communist call for repairing dykes against tidal waves.

Another course of rural dissatisfaction is the communist regimentation policy, which in many of its aspects is contrary to traditional Chinese concepts of life, such as the policy of forming village women into societies and the frequent meetings which the farmers are obliged to attend.

Because of the communist news blockade, very little independent information has leaked out regarding the conditions in the rural districts in the so-called "old liberated areas" (areas ruled by the communists since the Sino-Japanese War). Communist propaganda claims that the standard of living in these areas has been uplifted and the farmers are a happy lot.

The only independent information I collected regarding these areas was that given by friends. One friend visited many villages in the "old liberation areas" about forty miles south of Tientsin on wheat-buying trips. He found conditions in all the villages he had visited the same. There were no houses with tiled roofs. All houses had straw roofs and were in a dilapidated state with holes in the walls. They looked as if no one had lived in them for years. He asked one farmer why. The farmer told him, "If we have tiled roofs and repair our houses and make them look good, we will be in danger of being dubbed rich or accused of wasting money and labour on good living and neglecting production.

It was an age-old custom in these villages to have a travelling opera give performances several times a year in celebration of the harvest and other festivals. My friend found there were no more opera performances. A farmer told him, "When a travelling troupe performs here, no one goes to the show, because if we go we will be in danger of being dubbed a pleasure-lover, neglecting production".

One day he saw a man carrying water from a well a mile away from his home. The man made so many trips that my friend became curious. He reasoned that the man could not have needed so much water for his household use. Questioned, the man replied, "Our village *kanpu* ordered me to plant cotton instead of wheat this season. There is no rain. The *kanpu* told me to carry water from the well to water my cotton field. He said they do the same thing in Soviet Russia. Probably they do the same thing there, but maybe they do it with machine power, not human power".

The widespread disillusionment and discontent has been openly admitted by communist officials to be a serious problem. They charged that it is instigated by Kuomintang underground agents. It is conceded that the charge contains some truth, but neutral observers maintain that communist policies are largely responsible.

Rural discontent has helped in the operation of anti-communist forces, such as the Ninth Route Army and other so-called "Anti-Communist National Salvation Columns". Some of these forces were formed spontaneously by the discontented farmers, some independently by Kuomintang stragglers and some were left behind by the Kuomintang Army Command.

Many communist-held cities in the outlying districts are blockaded by resistance forces in much the same way as Kuomintang armies were enclosed in cities by rural communist forces in former days. In the Tungliu district in northern Kiangsi, rural hostility was so tense that the communist *hsien* magistrate dared not leave the city without a heavy guard, according to travellers from there.

11. Problems Facing the Communists – Currency

The Chinese communists' people's currency, *renminbi*, which communist propaganda claims "will definitely not depreciate", appears to be heading in the same direction as the nationalists' gold yuan.

The communist claim stood its ground remarkably well during the first few months following the liberation of Nanking and Shanghai when there was relatively surprising economic stability. Credit was given by observers to effective communist economic control; however, these observers maintained that relative stability was also a sign of business depression obtained after communist occupation of the Nanking-Shanghai area. As the communists expanded their territorial control, resulting in a partial recovery of business, stability broke down and inflationary conditions appeared similar to those which had existed under the nationalists. The first violent fluctuation of prices which started after the communist capture of Canton continues today.

Prices are now jumping once, sometimes twice a day, sometimes once in every three days and sometimes once a week. It is estimated that prices have soared forty to eighty times since the communists took over Nanking and Shanghai. People are beginning to carry their money in a bag to pay for dinner. Unofficial interest rates in Shanghai are now fluctuation 150 to 320 percent per month. Public utility rates are readjusted frequently.

During the first four months after the liberation of Nanking and Shanghai, the largest denomination note in circulation was RMB$200. In August, notes of RMB$500 and RMB$1,000 were introduced. Soon notes of RMB$5,000 and RMB$10,000 will also be put into circulation, according to an informed source. The Central Mint in Shanghai is now working twenty-four hours a day and its production of notes is said to be four times the production under the Kuomintang. The total note issue is, however, kept secret.

Black market dealings in foreign currencies and gold and speculation in commodities have reappeared, but on a smaller scale than during the Kuomintang days. At times it is so rife that official foreign exchange rates have become unrealistic. The black market rate for American dollars is sometimes thirty to fifty percent higher than the official rate.

Price fluctuations are causing grave concern to the communist government. Chief anti-inflationary measures which they have enforced since they came into Shanghai and Nanking are cutting down government expenditures to the barest minimum, making public services self-supporting and imposing high taxes and levies on business, industrial and agricultural production. Neutral observers maintain that current economic instability is in no way a reflection on the efficiency of the communist government, which is generally considered to be of a much higher standard than that of the nationalists. The communist government has achieved considerable success in its anti-inflationary nature. It is especially successful in its anti-extravagance drive, making it less necessary for the government to resort to the printing press than was necessary during the nationalist days. It has made a much better showing than its predecessor in controlling private hoarding, speculation and other types of illegal trading. But, in the opinion of competent economic observers, the problem is more one of a gradual process of economic recovery than one of control.

Officially, the communists have conceded that inflation will continue for the next few years. No. 2 communist leader Liu Shao-chi said in a recent speech that 1950 would be the most trying year economically for the government. Finance minister Ho I-po in his budget speech on December 2 revealed that 61.6 percent of the budgetary deficit, which is 18.7 percent of the total budget, would be met by the printing press. The communists committed a serious political blunder in claiming that their people's currency, unlike the Kuomintang's gold yuan which they dubbed a "public swindle", is inflation-proof. Communist propaganda energetically pressed its claim during the few months of economic stability, reminding the people frequently through their newspapers, "I told you so. The people's currency will definitely not depreciate".

Last October inflation of a violent nature set in, and the communists were put on the spot. Their propaganda with their usual "Ah Q" (a character of self-deceit immortalised by famous Chinese novelist Lu Hsun in his novel "The Biography of Ah Q") spirit tried to defend its former claim by explaining that the upward fluctuation of prices nowadays, unlike that prevalent under the Kuomintang, which was a "sign of economic collapse", is an "inevitable by-product of victory". It would help in bringing about economic prosperity, in increasing production and the interflow of goods between urban and rural areas. This is the theme of Premier Chou En-lai's speech and of an official report on economic conditions made in Peking in November 1949.

The communist government, despite its propaganda claim, appears to have no confidence in its own currency, as evidenced by the fact it is collecting its taxes and levies and also paying its workers in some areas with rice or millet or parity units. Many Chinese took the communists at their word in regard to the people's currency. When inflation started and when communist propaganda resorted to its "Ah Q" spirit in trying to explain away the inflation, the public reacted very unfavourably. In Shanghai a popular comment is: "They are the same as the Kuomintang – just trying to bluff us".

The collapse of the people's currency, which neutral observers consider a good possibility, will be a thorny political problem for the communists when it comes, leaving aside its economic implications. Under the terms of communist ideology, anything that is the people's cannot, must not, and will not fail. Their policy is to call anything that is permanent the people's. When the time comes for a currency reform, their problem is, in the opinion of observers, what name should they give to the new currency?

12. Problems Facing the Communists – Agriculture and the Industry

Inflation will be the single biggest economic problem facing the Chinese communists for the next few years. Some other problems are:

Food shortage. Premiere Chou En-lai, in a directive to local communist authorities throughout the country on December 19, 1949, on how to cope with the food shortage problem, revealed that 100 million mows (approximately seventeen million acres) of cultivated land in China were damaged by floods, storms, droughts and pests in 1949 and food production was reduced by 12 trillion catties (approximately 7.3 million tons).

The directive said the worst affected areas are the East China area where about one-fifth (over fifty million mows) of the cultivated lands was destroyed, and Hopei province (where the communist capital of Peking is located) where thirty million mows were destroyed.

The flight of many farmers to the cities to avoid war ravages and heavy communist levies and taxes has left a wide expanse of fields uncultivated, especially in northern Kiangsu and southern Shantung. The "protest" action of farmers in Shantung of not fertilising their lands has also contributed to the lower agricultural output.

The high price of opium has induced many farmers, especially in northern Anhwei, to turn their rice fields into poppy fields. Several travellers from north of the Yangtse River told me that the communists are tacitly permitting poppy planting. I have also obtained conclusive proof that the Communist Trade Bureau is dealing in opium. Last August, travellers from Fowyang in northern Anhwei, where poppy is widely planted, said that opium was being sold at one-seventh the price prevailing in Nanking and other major cities. These travellers said the Communist Trade Bureau was one of the biggest buyers of opium in Fowyang. The Bureau shipped the opium to Nanking and made a huge profit.

Last summer a Communist Tax Bureau collector in Liuho was found guilty of corruption in connection with the sale of official opium. The collector came to Nanking with a consignment of opium and sold it on the black market. He pocketed the balance and bought himself a new khaki suit. When he returned to Liuho his new suit aroused the suspicion of his fellow *kanpus* and he was compelled to confess to the corruption in a mutual-criticism meeting.

A Nanking businessman, who made regular opium-buying trips north of the Yangtse River, told me that he was caught by the communists several times. Each time he was only asked to pay the taxes on the opium and was then released. The communists, however, told him he must send his opium to nationalist areas and sell it there.

The communist tacit concession to the opium trade is considered a realistic attitude. The communists are as anxious to eliminate opium-smoking as the nationalists. Their political stand is that opium-smoking cannot be eliminated by shooting people, but by a gradual process of education and persuasion. Under this policy, it means that opium-smoking would have to be permitted for some time and the communist calculation apparently is that since it is permitted, why not reap some income for the national treasury by taxiing and dealing in opium?

Unemployment and displaced citizens. No official estimate has been made of the number of people involved, but unemployment as a result of the change of government and the subsequent business depression and displacement of families by war and natural calamities appears very widespread, visible even to the most casual observer.

The communists have, for the purpose of easing the unemployment problem, abandoned the initial policy of discharging old nationalist-trained civil servants en masse and are now taking back discharged functionaries on the payroll; however, five men are being given the salary equivalent of three men.

The general problem of reviving industries and agriculture. The communists have achieved considerable success in some fields of production despite their meagre resources. In Manchuria, great strides are reported to have been made in industrial rehabilitation. In China proper, however, only an estimated twenty to forty percent of the factories have been reopened.

The nationalist port blockade is having a crippling effect on the programme for economic revival. In Shanghai, an informed source said most factories are now almost down to their last bale of cotton.

Industrial and agricultural revival is listed by the communists as next in importance to the military campaign for "liberating" the country. Unless living conditions of the general public are improved, discontent cannot be curbed nor communist rule consolidated.

In addition to the shortage of rice – China's staple food – there is also a grave lack of wheat and cotton.

Wheat. According to the *Takungpao*, flour mills in Shanghai are now operating ten days a month due to the shortage of wheat with the total output cut down to only 900,000 bags a month. In former days, the total monthly flour production in Shanghai was between two and three million bags. Seventy percent of the production normally goes to feed the flour-eating population in North China.

The paper said the mills are incurring heavy losses because they must pay regular wages to workers despite the fact that they are on half-production, which results in an increase in the cost of production. In August 1949, it was estimated the mills lost RMB$500 (US$0.03 according to the prevailing rate of exchange) on every bag of flour.

Cotton. Since the end of the Sino-Japanese War, the shortage of cotton has been the most serious problem in industrial rehabilitation. During the Kuomintang days, the United Nations Relief and Rehabilitation Administration (UNRRA) and later the United States Economic Cooperation Administration (USECA) aid helped tremendously in coping with the problem. Such outside aid is no longer available to the communists.

The communists in some areas in East and North China are compelling the farmers to plant cotton instead of rice to increase the supply of cotton, but it is apparently not being done on a large scale, as it cuts into the production of food which is also badly needed.

China normally requires fourteen million piculs to feed her 4.5 million spindles and rural handicrafts. Since the end of the Sino-Japanese war, China imported between sixty and eighty percent of her needs in cotton from America and other Western countries. This source of supply is no longer handy to the communists. Cotton-growing lands have been reduced from the pre-war peak area of

59.3 million mows to 37 million mows. These remaining mows are now producing at half their normal capacity, due to natural calamities and other factors.

It is generally agreed that the communists have the first essential for a speedy building of war-wrecked China – namely, an efficient, honest and energetic government which has shown its worth in the restoration of communications. Efficiency, honesty and energy in administration are, however, only a few of the essentials. There are others such as capital and popular cooperation, which the communists appear to be lacking in.

Because of the communist "lean to one side" foreign policy, it is apparent that China will have to pull herself up by her own bootstraps. Soviet Russia, with whom she is aligned, is generally presumed not to be in a position to grant her much help. The first deal she made with Soviet Russia was a barter trade agreement. The United States and other Western democracies, who are in a position to help, are not inclined to do so because of the hostile communist attitude. Pulling herself up by her own bootstraps will be a most difficult task, because it is the accepted view among observers that China, devastated by war and natural calamities almost continuously for the last four decades, is too weak economically to do so.

Because of the communist policy of eventually expropriating private property, the small Chinese money class generally has lost interest in long-term investment. The majority of them are sitting tight on their money, neglecting even repairs and improvements to their factories as was recently pointed out by the New China News Agency.

The communists are doing the utmost to drive these national industrialists out of their inertia. Though representing a class contrary to their ideology, the communists are admitting them into favour during the New Democracy period. One of the four small stars on the new national flag represents the national bourgeoisie class.

Li Chu-chen, general manager of the Tientsin Yungli Chemical Works, who is a prominent national industrialist and a "democratic personage", wrote an article in the *Takungpao* last August, advising his fellow-national industrialists to give up their lukewarm attitude and cooperate enthusiastically with the government in national reconstruction. Li said the New Democracy period would last for a long time, and exhorted them "not to worry about expropriation of private property".

The industrialists I talked to apparently are still unenthusiastic about long-term investments. The general comment among them is: "Why build a factory when one day it is to be taken away from us?"

The communists also make a political mistake in their radical practice of "struggling" with the rich in the rural areas. "Struggling" means dispossessing rich landlords of their money, land and other property and dividing these assets among the poor in the neighbourhood. This was done on a large scale in the old liberated areas and dissipated what would have been an important capital potential for reconstruction. The communists apparently have seen the disadvantages of this practice in relation to economic development. Their latest directive in regard to "struggling" provides that rich landlords be allowed to keep one-third of their cash assets on condition they invest it in industrial production.

13. Problems Facing the Communists – Famine

Communist China is now in the midst of a grave famine, affecting an officially-estimated forty million persons.

In a directive dated December 19, 1949, to local authorities on how to cope with the famine, Premiere Chou En-lai said seven to eight million of these affected persons are now "starving or half-starving". The directive described the famine as the "worst for the last few decades". It stressed to communist authorities throughout the country that the solution of this problem is vital to the consolidation of communist rule in China.

Premiere Chou En-lai said the worst affected areas are the East China provinces, where there are now sixteen million refugees and also Hopei province, where there are an estimated ten million semi-starving persons.

The directive called upon the local authorities to give priority to relief work. It suggested many relief measures, the most important of which is to organise the refugees into production units and make them work to relieve themselves.

Mao Tse-tung recently called upon communist army units similarly to form themselves into cooperative units, which offered handsome incentives for a boost in the production of food. Reliable sources estimate that thirty to forty percent of Red China's arable land has been damaged by droughts, floods and pestilence during the latter half of this year, while undamaged areas yielded only half of the normal crop. Reports from rural areas north of the Yangtse River said that even the most fortunate citizens were down to two meals of congee daily.

Many starving villagers are flooding the urban areas for food. Famine in the rural areas has caused the complete nullification of the Red's policy of dispersing "non-productive" residents from overcrowded Shanghai. The Reds have now abandoned this policy because every man sent back to the villages has returned to the city with many more. One of those returnees told me that he was unable to remain in his village because he had nothing to eat; he had to bring back his relatives because they, too, were starving.

Qualified sources said that there are approximately 120,000 starving and homeless refugees in Shanghai alone, with the authorities being unable to help. The number of beggars has risen sharply; they are found in every street and alley panhandling pedestrians and rickshaw passengers.

The famine has also caused widespread deterioration of public safety, with a sharp rise in the number of hold-ups and robberies. When I stopped at Nanchang for a few days, my train had arrived before dawn; the hotel was several miles away at the other side of the town. Railway attendants warned me to remain at the station till daylight instead of travelling to the city in the dark because of the prevalence of footpads and highwaymen. Police are virtually nonexistent.

Communist trade bureaus have succeeded in keeping the cities supplied with food, but the effects of the famine are beginning to creep into the urban areas, causing inflation and other dislocations. The New China News Agency admitted that famine was the primary cause of the violent price fluctuations last October and November, wherein the government dumped thousands of tons of rice and other commodities on the Shanghai market in an attempt to halt the runaway price spiral. (Recent economic reports inflated rice production one thousand to 1,500 percent within the past two months.)

Famine is considered one of the most serious problems the Reds have encountered in the consolidation of their political rule, and one which, in view of their foreign policy, will have to be solved without outside help. Soviet Russia, to whom the Chinese communists seem now definitely conjoined, is not only in no position to help, but has aggravated the situation by requiring shipments of Chinese food in exchange for Russian machinery under a one-year barter agreement.

The food situation in Manchuria appears to be slightly better than in China proper. Communist press reports said that Manchurian rice would soon be shipped to North China to help alleviate the famine, although this does not necessarily indicate a Manchurian surplus.

14. Problems Facing the Communists –
How to Sell Soviet Russia to the Chinese People

One big problem facing the Chinese communists in their programme of building a totalitarian China is how to sell Soviet Russia to the Chinese people.

Some observers consider this a basic problem. A Chinese "democratic personage" who spent several months in North China University – one of the many communist indoctrination camps – came to the conclusion that once a man has accepted Soviet Russia as not being an imperialistic power it would be easy for him to accept the rest of communist ideology.

Communist propaganda is at present mobilising all its resources and technique to make the Chinese people believe that Soviet Russia is not just China's only true friend, but also the only foreign country which can help rehabilitate and reconstruct China.

A National Sino-Soviet Friendship Association with branches in all major cities in China has been established. Membership of the association, according to the New China News Agency, has been boosted to over two million since its inception three months ago. Although this figure is probably correct, it should be noted that it was achieved by the compulsory *en bloc* enrolment of the members of other communist-controlled associations, such as the National Society of Writers and Artists.

Books on Soviet Russia are printed by the millions for sale to the general public at low prices. Soviet Russia, according to the Soviet cultural workers delegation which visited China recently, will send in six million more books to help in the "friendship" drive. Communist propaganda describes Soviet Russia as the country which was mainly responsible in defeating Germany and Japan in the Second World War, and also as the "liberator" of Manchuria, while it belittles America's part in the war. One popular claim of the communists is that Japan was forced to surrender due to Soviet Russia's ten day participation in the war and by the atomic bomb.

A movement has been initiated by top communist leaders, including Premier Chou En-lai and Chu Teh, to urge the people to learn from Soviet Russia. A recent incident in Peking showed, however, that communist leaders themselves also are in need of learning more about Soviet Russia.

When the Soviet cultural workers delegation arrived in Peking in October 1949, the crowd amassed by the communists to greet them sang a famous communist song to show their welcome. The song is called "You [the Communist Party] Are the Lighthouse". The communist leaders were surprised when the delegation told the communist leaders that the song should not be sung at welcome parties, because the tune was that of a funeral song composed for Lenin at his death. Messages were flashed immediately to all parts of the country ordering that the song not be sung anymore. The song was one of the first songs the communists taught school children to sing when they entered a new city. When the Soviet delegation arrived at Nanking, the welcome party was specially reminded not to sing the song. Photographs of Lenin and Stalin and Soviet flags are displayed in profusion in prominent places in the major cities. Communist newspapers run articles almost daily praising Soviet Russia even to the point of idolisation. Russian language is taught on the radio.

Present indications, however, show that the communists have not achieved much success in their Soviet friendship drive. The prevailing conceptions of the general public about Soviet Russia is that she is imperialistic vis-à-vis China and that she, among all the foreign countries, is least able to help in China's economic reconstruction.

The fact that Soviet Russia has wrested back many of the old Csarist imperialist rights in China which she had voluntarily renounced in 1924, and that she has removed US$2 billion worth of industrial equipment and materials from Manchuria, is common knowledge among the Chinese people. This fact is regarded as a big hurdle in the Soviet friendship drive. Questions regarding Soviet control of the Chinese Changchun Railway, Port Arthur and Dairen are often the first ones raised in meetings held by the communists to foster Sino-Soviet friendship.

These questions were raised even in communist indoctrination camps. According to one indoctrination camp cadre, the answer of the chief communist propaganda man in Shanghai, Fan Chang-chiang, was: "The interests of China and Soviet Russia in the world revolution are identical. Soviet control of the Changchun Railway, Port Arthur and Dairen is equivalent to China controlling them. Besides, Soviet Russia will eventually return them to China. Therefore, there is no cause for concern".

Another explanation made by other communist officials is that the Soviet Russian control of Port Arthur and Dairen is an essential security measure for the protection of both China and Soviet Russia against American "imperialism", and Soviet control of the Changchun Railway is essential in making her control of the two ports effective.

A communist newspaper in Nanking on October 16, 1949, printed an article giving an apologetic explanation to the Chinese people of Soviet Russia's control of the Changchun Railway. I am reproducing below the article in full to show the reasoning of the communists. The title of the article is: *How to Understand Soviet Russia; To Whom Is the Joint Sino-Soviet Control of the Changchun Railway Beneficial?* Its text is as follows:

> Everyone knows that the Changchun Railway was built by Russia. In 1889, the "country-seller" Li Hung-chang of the Manchu Dynasty signed a Russo-Chinese secret treaty giving the rights of building the Changchun Railway to csarist Russia.

> Csarist Russia built the Railway over a number of years with the sweat and blood of China's and Russia's labouring class. The Railway at that time was named the Chinese Eastern Railway.

> In 1919, after the Russian Revolution, the Soviet government voluntarily denounced all unequal treaties

which imperialist Russia had extracted from the weaker nations.

But the denunciation was ignored by the Peking government until 1924 when the Soviet Union sent an envoy by the name of Kalagan to Peking.

Kalagan concluded the Peking Convention with Dr. Wellington Koo, which allowed China to buy back the Chinese Eastern Railway and provided that prior to the purchase the railway should be jointly controlled by the two countries. (Originally it was controlled unilaterally by Russia.)

In 1945, Soviet Russia sent her armies into Manchuria and defeated the Japanese imperialists, wresting the Changchun Railway from the hands of the Japanese and returning it to the Chinese people.

For the sake of joint Sino-Soviet defence against our enemies and against the resurgence of Japanese imperialism, for the sake of facilitating the transportation of Soviet troops to Port Arthur during the war against Japan and for the sake of strengthening economic cooperation between China and Soviet Russia, the Sino-Soviet Changchun Railway Pact was concluded on August 14, 1945. The pact provided that the Railway shall be jointly controlled by the two countries for a period of thirty years within the framework of Chinese sovereignty.

With the cooperation of the labouring brethren of the Soviet Union, the labouring people of China have no fear of Japan or any other aggressor nations starting a second Mukden Incident [The Mukden Incident was the Japanese occupation of this Manchurian city on September 18, 1931, which marked the beginning of Japanese aggression against China]. Because of the Soviet defence of Port Arthur and because the powerful air, land and naval forces of the Soviet Union are fighting side by side with the Chinese People's Liberation Army, any war adventurer will be crushed.

The Railway is especially significant in relation to Soviet assistance in the economic reconstruction of China because during peace-time the Railway is purely a commercial transportation enterprise operated jointly by China and Soviet Russia. Not only does the Railway provide a link between the two countries, it pays taxes to the Chinese government according to Chinese taxation laws. Moreover, the pact also provides for the future restitution of the Railway with all its property to China at no costs.

Therefore, this Pact has a 'hundred benefits and not one harm' for the Chinese people.

As the situation stands today, it is correct to say that the communist Soviet friendship drive is being sneered at by the majority of the Chinese people. The communists seemed to concede this, too, as evidenced by their retreat in the promotion of the drive. Recently, the Communist High Command ordered that no Soviet flags or photographs of Lenin and Stalin be displayed except on occasions connected with Sino-Soviet relations. The *Takungpao* was reprimanded for printing Stalin's photograph to the left of Mao Tse-tung's photograph.

Though the Soviet friendship drive is an essential part of the communist political programme, a probable clue to its eventual outcome may be found in the reaction of many Chinese that they would be able to compromise with the Chinese communists, but never with Soviet Russia.

The communists conducted a survey of opinion in a Shanghai factory on which is the best and which is the worst foreign country. The majority answer from the workers was: America is the best foreign country because she gave them flour, and Soviet Russia is the worst because she wrested the Changchun Railway, Port Arthur, and Dairen from China.

The communist political director of a Shanghai middle school told a friend of mine that his biggest problem is how to find geography and history teachers for the school because the students always ask "embarrassing" questions regarding Soviet Russia in the geography and history classes. He said that he found one geography teacher after a long search, but the teacher soon quit because he could not answer the students' question of whether Outer Mongolia,

Port Arthur, and Dairen belong to China or to Soviet Russia.

The common belief among the majority of the Chinese population is that the Chinese communist drive to sell Soviet Russia to the Chinese people is bound to fail. There are too many inerasable historical memories and unbridgeable political differences for any long lasting harmony to be established between the two major communist countries. Soviet Russia, continuing the old csarist policies, has harmed Chinese sovereignty and territorial integrity in too many ways, on too many occasions and too grievously. What is now Soviet Russia's Far East, including the port of Vladivostok, was once Chinese territory which csarist Russia had annexed by force. Outer Mongolia, once an integral part of China, was detached and made an independent state, due to Soviet Russian pressure.

15. Soviet Help in the Sovietisation of China

Soviet Russian military and technical advisers are being despatched by the hundreds to Red China to help the Chinese communists Sovietise their country and assist its incorporation into the Soviet military strategy.

Soviet advisers are helping to plot the invasion of Taiwan, which will be launched in summer at the latest with land, sea, and air forces, according to authoritative communist informants. It is estimated that the Chinese communists will be able to muster at least one hundred fighting planes and thirty warships for the invasion of this last nationalist stronghold.

General Chen Yi, mayor of Shanghai, whose Third Field Army has been given the task of invading the island, is at present marshalling a select force of 180,000 men for this three-dimensional operation. This task force, concentrated around Shanghai and along the Chekiang coast, is undergoing special amphibious training.

One important part of the training programme is making the soldiers good sailors. About thirty miles north of Shanghai, the Chinese communists have erected an ingenious device consisting of nets supported upon high poles. Small groups of soldiers climb into the nets which are then rocked like a ship in order to accustom them to the sea motion.

Soviet instructors are also helping to train Chinese communist pilots and navy crews in Manchuria, according to informants. These sources said that about twenty Russian shipbuilders arrived in Shanghai last month to work in the Kiangnan Dockyards. Following the arrival of the Russians, several Americans employed by the dockyards, which were formerly operated under the Economic Co-operation Administration, were told to hand in the resignations.

A Russian-language nurses' training school has been established inside Shanghai in order to train Chinese personnel for service with the Soviet military missions. There are a number of such missions all over China, including at least one film unit which is filming strategic areas. This unit is accompanied by specially indoctrinated Chinese officers, whose task is to familiarise the Russians with China's defence problems. Most of the Soviet officers are at present stationed in Manchuria which has presumably been turned into a laboratory for testing the introduction of Soviet communists into China. Soviet missions can also be encountered in Shanghai and as far south as Canton.

Although there has never been any evidence of direct material Soviet aid to the Chinese communists, Manchurian observers believe that the Russians have supplied their Chinese allies with Japanese arms and replacement parts, made with the Japanese machinery which the Russian stripped from Manchuria and removed to within the Soviet border. An estimated 750,000 tons of Japanese arms have been turned over to the Chinese communists by the Russians.

One high-ranking Chinese "democratic personage" declared that the latest technical mission, which arrived in Manchuria recently, comprises of about three hundred experts. Another mission of about seventy Soviet railway engineers is attached to the Chinese communist railway repair corps.

The nine-arch steel bridge at Pengpu, fifty miles north of Nanking, has been repaired by Soviet engineers. The bridge, which spans the Hwai River, is one of China's most spectacular engineering feats and was originally designed and built by British engineers. It was badly damaged by the retreating nationalist troops in December 1948.

Chinese engineers who assisted the Soviet team said that Chinese and Russian engineers were segregated and that liaison was conducted through Chinese communist officials. The same source said that Soviet advisers are attached to the Health Ministry in Peking. Peking Radio recently reported that Russian doctors and scientists helped to combat the plague epidemic in Chahar province.

The source said that the Russians are taking special precautions to create a good impression among the Chinese. For example, in accordance with specific instructions from Stalin, members of the anti-plague corps wore Chinese communist army uniforms, lived in Chinese barracks and ate Chinese Liberation Army rations. Informed sources said that Russian engineers also helped to refloat the cruiser *Chungking* and the destroyer Chang Chih, which had been sunk by nationalist bombers after the crews had defected and sailed the vessels into communist ports. These vessels will presumably participate in the forthcoming invasion of Formosa. British-trained captain Teng Chao-hsiang, skipper of the *Chungking* when she defected to the communists in March, has been restored to his command of the cruiser.

16. Soviet Russians and Manchuria

The Soviet Russians appear to be disliked by the Chinese people in Manchuria. Chinese travellers from Manchuria said the people there nicknamed the Russians "Big Nose", as they had nicknamed the Japanese "Small Nose". They said a communist cartoonist once drew many caricatures of a foreigner captioned "American Big Nose Imperialist". In one of the captions, he forgot to insert the word "American". The Russians took offence and the cartoonist is now in an indoctrination camp.

The Russian language has now been made compulsory in all schools in the country. One communist-sponsored Chinese educational mission to Manchuria visited a primary school and asked the pupils whether they felt any differently towards studying Russian than they had towards studying Japanese during the old "Manchukuo" days. The pupils made a long face and declined to answer.

Dislike of the Russians has reportedly crept into the rank and file of the Communist Party itself. According to the communist propagandist, Liu Tse-ming, the anti-Soviet writings of Hsiao Chun, another communist journalist, had "some influence" on the younger members of the Party in Manchuria. Liu made this admission in a series of seven articles reprinted in the *New China Daily*, attacking Hsiao Chun for his charge against Soviet Russia of being imperialistic towards China. This controversy within the Communist Party was generally taken as confirmation of private information filtering into China Proper of the unpopularity of Soviet influence in China's rich Northeast.

The exact extent of Soviet domination in Manchuria is difficult to assess, but it must be very great, according to a popular belief among informed circles, because of Soviet control of the vital Changchun Railway and the terminal ports of Dairen and Port Arthur.

Manchuria is now designated a special area. I have seen a communist map in which Manchuria was coloured differently from the rest of China. Chinese may travel to any part of China with relative freedom, but travel to Manchuria is strictly controlled. A special permit must be obtained from local authorities with the approval of the Manchurian communists. Recently, the communists in Shanghai suspended the issuance of permits to visit Manchuria, citing the cold weather there as the reason.

Dairen and Port Arthur, which are virtually completely under Soviet domination, have been designated super-special zones. Travel restrictions to the two ports are even stricter than those applying to other parts of Manchuria. The Changchun Railway, which terminates at Port Arthur, does not maintain a direct service to the ports. The train runs only as far as Wulino, which is about fifty miles northwest of Dairen. The passengers must alight from the train, walk a short distance, show their permits to the Chinese communist and Soviet guards and then board another train for Dairen.

Manchuria is now being ruled along the lines of Soviet communism. All private property in the rural areas has been expropriated. Private property is still permitted in the urban districts, but is now being gradually squeezed out by large state monopolies and crippling taxes and levies. Private banks no longer exist there. According to the *Hsinminpao*, the ration between state and privately owned industries in Manchuria is now forty-eight to fifty-two. The production ratio this year of *kaoliang* is 10.24 million tons for state-owned to one million tons for privately owned industries.

The communists, along with Soviet technical assistance, have mapped out a three-year plan, which will begin in 1950 for the restoration of Manchurian industrial and agricultural production to the 1944 level. Li Fu-chun, vice chairman of the Manchurian people's government, said in a report on December 2 in Peking that thirty-five percent of the industries have been reopened thus far, but admitted actual production, especially of food, is "very low". Li said that communications have been completely restored and land reforms carried out throughout the country, but said the burden of farmers is still high, due to their being made to bear the brunt of financing the war of "liberation". According to Chinese travellers the farmers, like their counterparts in China Proper, are subject to heavy levies and taxes on their land production; this has reduced the farmers to a new low in poverty and a man possessing one ounce of gold is considered a rich man.

The New China News Agency reported on December 5 that commodity prices in Manchuria have risen only eighty percent during the whole of 1949 (compared with one hundred percent in other places). If this is true, it would seem that communist rule has at least brought economic stability to the Northeast. The communists in Manchuria are short of technical and skilled workers for their programme of industrial rehabilitation. Recently, several missions came to Nanking and Shanghai to recruit Chinese technicians, but less than two hundred trained engineers and workers responded to the call, although there are thousands of these people now jobless in the two cities. The main cause of this poor response is a general fear that once a man goes up to Manchuria he would find a job, but lose his individual freedom. In one recruitment meeting in Shanghai, the unemployed skilled workers asked that they be permitted to send an investigation mission to Manchuria before making a decision about going to work there.

Civil liberty in the Western sense has practically disappeared. The population has been regimented to work and produce for the state. Travellers said that the streets in most Manchurian towns are deserted except on weekends, the people being made to work all day long in the factories. Vice Chairman Li said the living conditions of the workers are improving, but admitted their salaries are still lower than those in China Proper.

The favourite communist weapon of travel restrictions has also been clamped on the people in Manchuria. A police permit must be obtained for even short-distance travels from one village to another. Anyone having an overnight guest at his home must report it to the police. Even people entering the hospital for medical treatment must do the same. In the Great Wall Pass of Shanhaikwan, the communists at one time even laid down regulations governing what time the people should go to bed and what time they should get up. People eating in restaurants or drinking tea in cafes or conversing in twos or threes are often questioned. Travellers said because of the necessity of getting photographers for the many police permits, photograph shops in Mukden are doing bristling business.

17. Moslem Opposition to Communist Rule

The Chinese communists are presently building a vast garrison of between 250,000 and 300,000 in the remote northwestern province of Sinkiang (which borders Russia) in order to reassert Chinese sovereignty over the virtually independent nomadic tribes, and also – according to a popular belief among Chinese communist circles – to "liberate" Tibet.

The Reds' position in the two northwestern provinces of Ninghsia and Chinghai is being shaken by the Moslem population, who are rising in armed opposition against Chinese communist rule, according to reports filtering to the coast. Communist workers who recently returned to Shanghai after a short term of service in the northwest said that of all the newly-occupied areas, the communists are encountering the stiffest hostility in Chinghai and Ninghsia.

The workers said the fight against the new rulers is conducted by Moslem civilians and soldiers formerly in the service of the Ma family, who "abdicated" rather than go along with the provincial command which joined the communists. These workers described Chinghai and Ninghsia as a "hornets' nest" of anti-communist resistance with numerous guerrilla forces roving the countryside, attacking communist communications, convoys and isolated garrisons.

They added that the predominantly Moslem population, which lived virtually in complete independence under the nationalists, is showing bitter racial hatred against the Chinese communists, whom they regard as "foreign invaders". Up to the present the Chinese communists have not been able to extend their control beyond a few main cities and the principal communication lines in Chinghai and Ninghsia. Conditions in Kansu are said to be much better because the Moslem population there is smaller. The vast countryside of Chinghai and Ninghsia is held by anti-communist guerrillas who are based deep in the mountains where they are using the supplies cached previously by the provincial army command.

The returned workers, who served under the communists but who are not Party members, said that uninformed communists in Sining, the capital of Chinghai, would not venture into the streets after five p.m., while guards patrolled the streets in groups of threes and fours. They said that one old Moslem man was arrested for having knifed three communist soldiers. On another occasion, four communist soldiers entered a Moslem home in the heart of the Sining city to fetch water, but only one emerged; the others had been murdered. A communist platoon searched the house and caught the murderers, but failed to find the bodies.

The Moslem populace is also resisting through their refusal to accept communist currency. Silver coins were still in circulation three months after the communist occupation. When compelled to accept the paper currency, Moslem shopkeepers retaliated by boosting prices sky-high.

The workers said that the communists are countering hostility with a policy of extreme forbearance and leniency, which they believe is the best means of pacifying the country. Killers are being shown extreme leniency and are executed only after repeated offences.

Three specially organised transportation corps, each numbering seven to eight hundred trucks, have been engaged since October 1949, in moving the vast army into Sinkiang. The troops are moved over the Lanchow-Urumchi highway through a two-hundred-mile waterless stretch of the Gobi Desert. The convoys are heavily guarded because of rampant guerrilla activities. The drivers said that the communists told them they would be given another mission after the completion of the troop movement into Sinkiang. They presumed this meant moving troops for the "liberation" of Tibet, which is more accessible through Sinkiang. They said that the troops are also being moved into Sinkiang in an attempt to end the resentment among local troops, who were ordered to be reorganised into the regular communist army. Until November 1949, the transportation corps moved 150,000 on to Sinkiang, bringing back heavy artillery and anti-aircraft guns captured from the Moslem troops.

18. Foreigners in Communist China

The Chinese communist policy towards foreigners appears to be to edge them out of China – at least from the interior.

A number of foreign missionaries, after observing communist rule for the past few months, are given to pessimism as regards the future. One prominent American missionary told me that the Chinese communists, although avowedly guaranteeing freedom of religious belief, are out to eliminate freedom of religious action. He said that the first blow against the Church has already been struck by the Chinese communists who closed eighty percent of the rural churches in Shantung province and over fifty percent in Manchuria and Hopei. Officially, the Shantung churches were sealed because they were "private organisations" which are not permitted to exist, although no official reason has been given for the closures in Manchuria and Hopei.

A similar policy seems to be followed as regards foreign businessmen, despite Mao Tse-tung's assertions that the communists welcome foreign trade. According to all indications, the communists do not intent to expel the foreigners officially, but make life so difficult that they would leave voluntarily.

One of the handiest weapons is travel restrictions, whereby foreigners living in the coastal cities are not permitted to visit outstations or make business visits to other cities. For example, the British manager of a large export firm in Nanking was unable to take his home leave because the communist authorities did not allow his colleague in Hankow to travel to Nanking to replace him. His colleague was told that he could have a permit to leave the country any time, but not one permitting transfer from one city to another.

Most foreigners believe that in the future they will be permitted to continue in business, but only in the larger cities and ports, where they would do all the buying and selling. They also believe that they will not be permitted to travel in the interior or maintain branches there after the present staff leaves. They believe that foreign firms with large properties in the interior of China – mostly British – will eventually be compelled to sell out to Chinese interests.

Missionary informants said that they have protested to Premier Chou En-lai against the closure of the churches in Shantung, Manchuria and Hopei. Premier Chou En-lai replied that the government would investigate, but no official action has been taken to reopen the churches. Some congregations have not been interfered with, while others are required to follow various regulations. Religious instruction has been banned in some missionary schools, but elsewhere it is allowed to continue as a voluntary course.

In addition to the closing of churches, the Chinese communists are also restricting the activities of missionaries. Some missionary sources said that this may be designed to eliminate foreign influence, while permitting the indigenous clergy to remain. At the present time, the Church has no legal standing and some missionaries were told that they will have no legal standing as long as foreigners remain on the mission staff.

Travel restrictions are placed on foreign missionaries as well as on foreign businessmen. Some missionaries in Anhwei province were not allowed to travel to Nanking even for medical treatment; however, they are being allowed to leave China altogether. Missionaries in Manchuria are not allowed to move at all. Missionaries who left their stations for other places or on home leave before communist occupation are not permitted to return to their stations. American missionaries in Nanchang were questioned by communist police whether they were agents of the American government.

Apparently, a great deal of authority is placed in the hands of local administrators, who administer regulations in a number of different ways. In areas where the communist officials are of a good nature, the missionaries receive kind treatment. In Chuhsien, about thirty miles north of Nanking, there is even a little fraternisation between communist *kanpus* and missionaries. Illiterate communists pay friendly visits to missionary homes and ask the missionaries to teach them to read. In other places, missionaries are subjected to unruly treatment. For instance, in Kuling, the famous summer resort in northern Kiangsi province, American pastors are sometimes not permitted to preach.

Chinese pastors are also finding life difficult under the communists. In Chenkiang, fifty miles east of Nanking, Chinese pastors are required to register with the police and are questioned extensively about their attitude towards the communist government, their connection with the United States and how they get their financial support.

Other types of foreign establishments subject to suspicion are the Rotary Clubs. All Rotary Clubs in the Yangtse valley, except in Nanking and Shanghai, have been compelled to disband. Wusih Rotarians were questioned at their weekly luncheons. The YMCA at Nanchang, Kiangsi province, was searched and files and documents examined in order to ascertain its connection with the American government.

Communist treatment of foreign diplomats is particularly unconventional and unfriendly. When the communists came into Nanking and Shanghai, they refused to recognise the diplomatic status of the ambassadorial and consular representatives of the foreign governments. They even refused to establish any kind of relations with the foreign consulates, which is contrary to a widely-accepted international practice.

Dr. J. Leighton Stuart, American Ambassador to China, told me that the communists in this respect were presumably following the Soviet Russian model.

After the communists came into Shanghai and Nanking, all the foreign ambassadors and consuls became "former ambassadors and consuls". They are required to sign as such in their communications with the communist authorities. A comic note was struck when the communists made the Dutch Ambassador and his wife sign a police document as "the former Dutch Ambassador Baron van Aerssen and the former Missus van Aerssen".

An incident occurred when Mr. Walun Konchon, Secretary of the Siamese Embassy in Nanking, applied to the police for a travel permit for the Siamese Ambassador to go down to Shanghai to board the American evacuation ship *General Gordon* for home. As the *Gordon* was originally scheduled to arrive at Shanghai on August 27, 1949, Mr. Konchon applied for a permit for the Ambassador to go to Shanghai on August 21. Two hours after he was given the permit, information came from Shanghai that the ship would arrive on August 23. He rushed down to the police station and requested that the date on the permit be altered to August 18.

The police officer refused to change the date. Konchon pleaded and argued with the officer for two hours, maintaining that nothing would be simpler than changing the date, but had no success. He finally lost his temper and shouted at the officer, "Now, listen! There are only a few Siamese in Nanking, but there are over two million Chinese in Siam!" The police offer then granted his request.

19. "Democratic Personages" in Peking

When Mao Tse-tung moved his headquarters last spring from a village outside Shihchiachuang to Peking, one of the first things he did was to summon the many so-called "democratic personages" and leaders of democratic parties to a meeting.

Mao asked them whether they were joining in the communist government as hosts or guests. He explained that as hosts, they would have to accept the leadership of the Communist Party, but as guests they would be accorded an honoured reception. The thing which Mao did not say, but which all those present understood, was that as guests they would not be given any share in the political party. The "democratic personages", according to a communist source, replied that they were joining in as hosts. This settled the relationship between the Communist Party and its political supporters. From that day onwards, the democratic parties virtually lost their own individual political identity.

The Democratic League abandoned its platform for parliamentary democracy. The "democratic" factions of the

Kuomintang accepted the communist form of government, although it ran counter in many fundamental aspects to Sun Yat-sen's Three People's Principles. Li Chi-sen and other anti-Chiang Kai-shek Kuomintang leaders still talk of implementing Sun Yat-sen's principles in China, but in all parts of the country the first communist directive to schools is to scrap his teachings from the curriculum.

I once interviewed a prominent leader of a democratic party. Asked whether he honestly thought the communist government is democratic and that there is real freedom of the press, he replied, "Please don't ask me any embarrassing questions". He requested me not to publish anything he said in the interview, but said he would be willing to say something for publication if written questions were submitted. "But," he still hastily added, "please don't include any embarrassing questions".

The democratic parties and "personages" are consulted in all political issues, but their opinions are only sometimes accepted. Informed sources said that in all basic matters the communist point of view always prevails. This accounts for the fact that, although the democratic parties and "personages" were known to have held divergent views on many political matters, the common administrative programme and form of government approved by the recent People's Political Consultative Conference in Peking were almost exactly as the communists had previously said they would be.

The "democratic personages" are now grouped into a large galaxy of about fifty political factions and parties. According to a leader of the Kuomintang Revolutionary Committee, the communists had expressed the "hope" that they would integrate themselves into only two major parties around the Kuomintang Revolutionary Committee and the Democratic League, as the Kuomintang factions had already carried out the communist "hope".

I asked a democratic party leader who had just returned to Nanking from the PPCC meeting in Peking whether the democratic parties would in future be permitted to conduct political campaigns in elections and to canvass new members on their own political platforms. He replied that on the basis of communist ideology this would not be possible. Communist ideology, he said, is that now that the "people" have come into power there is no longer any necessity for parties or political campaigning.

The "democratic personages" in Peking are treated like royal guests. They live in the best hotels and houses and are given the best food. But, according to travellers from Peking, they have virtually lost their freedom. They cannot say or do as they wish, but only as the communists have directed. In theory they are partners or co-operators in the new regime, but in actual practice their role is more of political subordinates. They are heavily guarded and are not free to see anyone they like. Friends or relatives visiting them are cross-examined by the communist gate office in a manner to discourage further visits. When the "personages" receive visitors in their hotel rooms, the hotel boys come in with tea or cigarettes every minute to check on what they are talking about.

Once, a close associate of a top leader of a democratic party arrived in Peking from Hong Kong. He approached the communist gate office at the Peking hotel for permission to see the leader. The gate office asked him a myriad of personal questions and told him to come the next day. When he called at the office the next day, he was told that the leader was busy and would not have time to see him. He called at the office again two days later, but was told that the leader was out. At that moment the leader's wife coincidentally appeared at the door of the hotel. She saw the man and immediately waved him in. The wife led him into their room and there sat the leader. The man asked the leader to help him find a job. The leader said he could not do that, but that he could give him a recommendation to join a communist "university" for indoctrination, after which he would be given work by the communists. The man asked the leader about conditions in new China. The leader's wife broke in, "Conditions? We are waiting for a new emperor". Then, pointing to her husband, she added, "You fellows are now running wild". The leader put his finger to his lips: "Please, be cautious in what you say".

The "democratic personages" spend practically all their waking hours attending communist meetings, meetings of the government and meetings for learning communist ideology, which leaves them with very little or no time for personal affairs. Some of the "democratic personages" have their homes in Peking, in line with the communist austerity drive that they should remain in their homes and have their meals there to save money for their national treasury. They are all required to live in communist-controlled hotels or hostels. Professor Chang Hsi-yo and Fei Hsiao-tung, who are two of those who have homes in Peking, are required to stay in the Hotel de Pekin. This segregation is apparently made to ensure proficient communist supervision of their movements.

The "democratic personages" are apparently dissatisfied with their position. As one of them admitted, the cause of democracy for which they had been fighting is now lost, yet there is the consolation of a little authority in the government instituted by the communists and the hope of the communists changing, in the course of time, to be more democratic. This "personage" maintained that "democratic personages" can more effectively persuade the communists to the cause of democracy by participating in the communist government than by remaining outside in opposition.

This is not the way the communists view things. The communists are adopting an attitude of extreme tolerance towards the "democratic personages". They are taking in anyone of political or financial influence regardless of his past record or political beliefs as long as he publicly avows wholehearted support for them. Communist calculations apparently are that it is better to take them in than to leave them outside, because when left outside they may become enemies. Besides, their collaboration is needed to compensate for the shortage of administrative personnel and the lack of administrative experience of the Communist Party.

This policy of taking in "democratic personages" is distasteful to the rank and file of the Communist Party. Power-ranking communist *kanpus* have openly protested against it. In one meeting in Peking Mao Tse-tung singled out the protest for a special reprimand. He said that *kanpus* who complained that "to be an old revolutionary is not as good as to be a new revolutionary and to be a new revolutionary is not as good as to be a non-revolutionary" displayed a lack of understanding of the party's policy, and added that at present a united front with other parties is of the utmost importance in the reconstruction of the country.

The rank and file of the Communist Party view the "democratic personages" with contempt and term them "opportunists". A woman in Nanking who was invited to join the Democratic League was advised by her communist friends not to accept, because once she joined the League she would be looked upon as an "opportunist" and it would be difficult for her to continue in public life.

One communist member in Shanghai gave the following instances showing why the "democratic personages" are not well-liked by his comrades:

(1) Shi Liang, a leader of the Democratic League, took over a factory in Tientsin from a friend who had left for Hong Kong. The factory included "bureaucratic capital" and should, according to communist law, be confiscated. But Shi Liang proclaimed it the property of the Democratic League and the communist city government was unable to touch the factory.

(2) The communist Sanlien Book Publishing House in Mukden was printing the complete works of the famous Chinese novelist Lu Hsun. Lu Hsun's wife, Hsu Kwang-ping, who is a "democratic personage", asked the Sanlien for royalty amounting to 170 bars of gold. The Sanlien asked the Communist High Command in Peking for a decision. The High Command approved the royalty. The Sanlien then offered to pay the approved royalty in Manchurian currency, but she refused and asked for gold bars instead. The Sanlien again asked the High Command for a decision. The High Command approved payment in gold bars.

(3) The "democratic personages" refused to cooperate in the recent austerity drive. They are given more

automobiles than top communist leaders, live in the best hotels and are given the best food. When the communists once gave them third-grade food in line with the austerity drive, they protested by not eating. The next day the communists were compelled to switch back to *shiao chao* (first-grade food) for them.

20. Will the Communists Turn Titoists in the Future?

The most frequently discussed question among both Chinese and foreign circles in communist China is whether the Chinese communists will remain as they are or change to be more democratic or turn Titoists in the future.

Opinion on this is divided and both sides seem to have cogent reasons for their beliefs. However, all the communists I talked to replied with an emphatic "no" when asked if they would turn Titoists in the future.

After studying communist rule for eight months, in the course of which I talked to a wide variety of sources representing all walks of life, including communists and "democratic personages", I have arrived at the following observations regarding the future of communism in China:

The Chinese communists are here to stay, at least for the next few decades. They have gained national power the hard way, and there is nothing that the Kuomintang or any other influence can do to oust them.

The Chinese communists will succeed in China, but not communism. Communism in many of its aspects is known to be unsuitable to Chinese conditions and life. The communists in many ways have already found that out, even during the short time of national rule.

In the People's Political Consultation Conference held in Peking in September 1949, the Communist High Command overruled suggestions from communist delegates that the aims of socialism and internationalism – alignment with communists in other countries for world revolution against the capitalistic nations – be written into the Common Administrative Programme.

The High Command's explanation for the overruling was that socialism is definitely the policy of the government and needs no further reiteration, and that patriotism mentioned in the Programme implies internationalism. Political observers, however, maintain that the overruling was made as a concession to public feeling.

The Chinese communists must change or fail. The majority opinion among the Chinese people regarding the communists is that they are both good and bad and though the good is more than the bad, the bad is at the most fundamental places. In other words, the communists possess the attractions for popular support – that is, chiefly their sponsorship of the underdogs and their comparatively efficient and clean administration. But they incur widespread dissatisfaction with their "lean to one side" ideology – that is, totalitarianism in internal policy and unconditional alignment with Soviet Russia in foreign policy.

One impression I had of communist rule is that they are now regarded by the majority of the people as something alien to China, probably due to the many un-Chinese methods of government adopted by the communists. In practically all government offices and other organisations, communist and non-communists are segregated mentally and psychologically. Non-communists always refer to their communist colleagues as "they". I asked several bystanders in a street in Shanghai after a nationalist air raid for their reactions towards the bombing. They replied, "They don't come to bomb us". This, according to long-time residents, is the way the people spoke when Chinese planes bombed the city when it was under Japanese occupation. It seems, therefore, that if the Chinese communists want to consolidate and retain their political hold on the country, which in the final analysis is what any political party values most, they must change.

The Chinese communists have succeeded in China, but democracy has not failed, because any change which would be made by the communists will inevitably be towards democracy.

Some foreign circles in communist China are of the opinion that any change that were to come about would only come after a split within the Communist Party. Splits are typical in political parties, and there is a possibility that it will happen within the Chinese Communist Party. Informed Chinese circles believe that a cleavage will not be possible as long as Mao Tse-tung lives. Mao is now the undisputed leader of the party. According to "democratic personages", he is worshipped like a god by communist members who regard him as not only a political, but also a military genius since he, and not Army Commander Chu Teh, is the mastermind who plans all the major campaigns.

Furthermore, there are no opposing factions within the Communist Party powerful enough to start a controversial split. The new government is dominated by what informed Chinese quarters call the "Yenan *Kanpu* Faction", that is, the members who were trained by Mao Tse-tung during the old Yenan days. The other group inside the party, known as the International communists headed by Li Li-san, is now out of power.

Mao Tse-tung is considered by some "democratic personages" as a rightist-minded realist. These quarters who, like the common man in China, are also wishing for a change in the communist policy, are pinning their hopes on Mao, despite the fact that Mao, like the other communist leaders, is at present talking and acting in a strictly ideological way.

To substantiate their confidence in the realism of Mao Tse-tung, one of the "democratic personages" cited the following incident: One night during the Peking peace negotiation days last April, Mao Tse-tung and members of the communist and nationalist delegations were relaxing after a reception dinner. Someone raised the question of why Chiang Kai-shek had collapsed so quickly. Mao Tse-tung immediately offered an answer. He said that Chiang collapsed so quickly because he "always wants to mah-jong thirteen heads in a mah-jong game". Thirteen heads is a winning head consisting of the first and last characters in the various suits. It fetches a high stake, as it is extremely difficult to attain. By thirteen heads, Mao also meant that Chiang's policy was to make every one of his chief subordinates head of a faction and make the different factions oppose each other to create a balance of power.

Mr. Chang Shih-chao, one of the nationalist peace delegates retorted, "Yes, it is not right for Generalissimo Chiang always to want to mah-jong thirteen heads, but Chairman Mao, you must not always want to mah-jong one of the same suit". This, too, is a difficult-to-attain high streak winner. By "one of the same suit", Chang Shih-chao was referring to the communist "lean to one side" policy.

To this Mao replied, "Mr. Chang, you have over-estimated me. My practice is, when I can mah-jong, I mah-jong".

Some circles are sceptical whether the Chinese communists will be able to shake off Soviet Russian domination once it is established to pave the way for a change in foreign policy. Other quarters, however, maintain that the question is whether Soviet Russia will be permitted to establish such a hold on China as to make it difficult for the communists to shake it off. These quarters point out that the Chinese communist revolution is nationalistic in its fundamental nature and aims, and most of the people joining in the revolution did so more for reasons of patriotism than because of their belief in Marxism.

There were two periods of rapid growth of the Chinese Communist Party – one after the outbreak of the Sino-Japanese War and the other after V-J Day. When the communists settled down in Yenan after the six-thousand-mile Long March in 1936, the Party's membership totalled less than fifty thousand. After the outbreak of and during the Sino-Japanese War, membership leapt to 900,000. After V-J Day, it rose to the present high of three million.

This means that most people joined the Communist Party to fight the Japanese and out of disgust with the nationalists' misgovernment, not out of belief in communism. Of course, after they joined the Party they were thoroughly indoctrinated with communist ideology. The question here is whether a man can be made to permanently forget his primary motive and ideals by later indoctrination, especially after he has come from the village to the city. The communists did not win as communists;

but rather as crusaders against nationalist misgovernment and degeneration. As one high-ranking communist once observed in a private conversation, "It's not that we won, but that the Kuomintang lost".

Communist political slogans, which aroused the most popular support, are not communistic in nature. In fact, communist ideological opposition against landlordism and capitalistic exploitation is rarely seen in the slogans. The most commonly used slogans are against nationalist misgovernment, corruption, bureaucratic capitalism and one-party dictatorship. In other words, the communist success in China is not a victory of ideology but one over nationalist misgovernment. The communists have popular support in fighting the Kuomintang, though it remains to be seen whether they can successfully sell their ideology to the Chinese people.

Final success depends largely on how far the communists will go to satisfy the traditional and deeply-rooted Chinese conceptions of life. What the people want most is a life of freedom and a chance to maintain that life, with as little interference from the government as possible.

Because of their "lean to one side" foreign policy, the communists are expected to have a difficult time bringing about sufficient economic reconstruction to ensure a decent livelihood for the people. Even if they succeed after a period of hardships in uplifting the people's standard of living, they will find it difficult to give the people a reasonable amount of freedom to live due to their totalitarian policies. When it comes to fighting against the traditional concepts of life, the communists will most probably find the people much more difficult to conquer than the Kuomintang.

One question in the minds of many observers is: Yes, there are compelling factors for a change of communist policies, but will the stubbornly-ideological communists change of their own accord or will outside pressure, such as rebellions, uprisings and organised political opposition, be necessary? In my opinion, outside pressure will be necessary.

In light of current communist policies and the pronouncement made by their leaders and propaganda, it would seem there is little hope for a democratic switch by the communist government. However, Chinese circles point out that communists are now at the moment of victory and it is, therefore, natural that they should talk and act in strict conformity with the ideology for which they had been fighting for the last twenty-two years. When the communists come face to face with the real problems of ruling a vast country like China with difficulties cropping up one after another, they will have to think twice before they talk and act.

Though the communists have conquered almost the entire country, the real administrative problems have not yet appeared in full force; and the situation has already proved a tough one for the communists. There is grave famine, inflation, industrial and agricultural stagnation and widespread disillusionment and discontent with communist rule, for which the communists have not yet produced any effective remedies.

Those problems have already forced the communists to abandon some of their old methods of government which they had employed when their control was confined mainly to rural areas. The change lies in their more liberal attitude towards the money class.

The communists have also failed in the implementation of three important policies during their short period of national power: (1) austerity in administrative expenses and the employment of administrative personnel; (2) the dispersal of the non-productive people from the cities; and (3) the removal of industries from Shanghai to the interior. These policies were presumably mapped out in a village conference room for later enforcement in the cities, without a foretaste of urban difficulties.

The problem of political pacification of the country after military conquest will soon demand urgent treatment and solution. There will be many more problems, the solution of which will call for something more than the resources now at the disposal of the Chinese communists. Foreign assistance will be necessary in coping with some of the problems, and the Chinese communists will probably come to the first realisation of their mistake in aligning solely with Soviet Russia.

There is an abundance of evidence that the Chinese communists have found, and will continue to find, their newly-gained national power difficult to digest in the next few years. The force of circumstances, to which the average communist throughout the world is particularly sensitive, may prove a compelling factor in the moderation of their policies. The majority of the Chinese people are also finding radical communist rule difficult to digest. The widespread disillusionment and dissatisfaction are considered to be consequent upon the communists being too harsh on the people economically and politically.

This harshness is dictated by communist ideology, and unless there is a policy change, political pacification of the country will be a difficult task for the communists. It is generally believed that the communists will find the task of political pacification more difficult than that of militarily overthrowing the Kuomintang because indications show that they are lacking in the kind of popular support in the enforcement of their political rule, which they admittedly had in the military fight against the Kuomintang.

Some of the disgruntled professors in communist China have come to consider the communists just as counter-revolutionary as the Kuomintang in light of Dr. Sun Yat-sen's principles, which have been accepted as gospel by the Chinese people. These professors pointed out that although the communists are obviously instituting economic socialism, they are denying the people a democratic form of government, which is one of Dr. Sun's chief principles. They are also of the belief that unless the communists changed there will probably be another revolution in China. One Nanking professor, a former communist sympathiser who later joined the ranks of the disillusioned, said that the Chinese people would reject a communist government if they were allowed to vote freely.

21. Farewell to Communist China

The Chinese communists banned the foreign press in Nanking on October 1, 1949, in the most unusual manner. We were not informed in any way that we were banned, and had to go to the communists and goad them into telling us that we were.

On September 25, the Nanking telegraph office suddenly stopped accepting our press messages. When asked why, the office clerk said he did not know, but was just following directions from the superior authorities. I was at a loss as to what this suspension of our press cable privilege meant. Had we been banned, or could we still write mail copy and send stories by commercial cable? I went to the Communist Foreign Affairs Bureau on September 30 to make inquiries, where I was received by a Mr. Tsui, who could not answer my questions. He said he would check with the higher authorities for clarification and let me know later.

I went home and immediately wrote a story on my talk with Mr. Tsui. On October 1, I showed the story to Mr. Tsui for him to check whether the contents were correct before I filed it. Mr. Tsui read my story and looked as if he were a bit perturbed. He told me to wait and left the room. After ten minutes I was led into another room. A communist official came in and started asking me detailed personal questions as if he were cross-examining a criminal suspect. After he was through with the "cross-examination", he asked me what my business was. He had my story with him and obviously knew what I had come for. Nevertheless, I politely told him that I had come to show a story to Mr. Tsui before filing it. He said his office was not responsible for checking foreign correspondents' stories. I told him I realised it was not his responsibility, but to correspondents it was a matter of etiquette that when they wrote an interview they showed it to the interviewee to determine whether the contents were correct before filing it.

I asked whom he was. He said he was Huang Hua, Director of the Foreign Affairs Bureau. I then said, "What I am after is just to find out whether the suspension of our press cable privilege means that we were banned or not. Mr. Tsui couldn't not tell me. Can you tell me?"

Huang replied, "It means that you and all other foreign correspondents in Nanking are banned from further reporting activities. You may stay here as a private citizen. You were registered with the reactionary Kuomintang government, which we cannot recognise".

My reply was, "Fine, that's all I want to know. I don't care about the banning, but why were we not informed that we were banned?" He did not answer my question. I then told him there was also an Associated Press correspondent in town and that he should inform him. Huang said, "We have no need to inform him". I pointed out that if the AP man were not informed he might continue to "violate your ban and you may put him in gaol". I asked whether I could tell the AP man to come to see him for the verbal ban. He again said, "You have no need to do that. He would know somehow". The first thing I did upon reaching home was to pass the news to the AP correspondent, so that he would not unknowingly continue to violate the press ban and get himself into trouble.

The Shanghai communists banned the foreign press in a more "decent" manner on October 7, 1949, with an official announcement in the papers. After we were banned, I immediately applied to the communist police for a permit to go to Hong Kong. I was worried when the communist clerk to whom I presented my application shook his head and told me, "A travel permit to other parts of liberated

China, you can get easily. But one to Hong Kong is going to be a little difficult because Hong Kong has not yet been liberated".

Later, however, I found that the reception clerk was talking wishfully. The high communist authorities, to whom my application was referred, granted me the permit in the most polite manner. The head of the Third Section of Nanking's Public Safety Bureau, who handled my application, came out to ask me to get the applicant to come personally. I told him that I was the applicant. He then told me to come back the next day to get my permit. He must have known my name from my despatches which, along with the news service of the other foreign wire services, were monitored by the communists who have them translated for study by their *kanpus* in their almost daily political sessions. He had thought I was a much older man. I was then thirty-three. The next day I returned to his office, but my permit was not yet ready. He told me to wait and went personally to the typewriter office to instruct them to type out my permit. I waited for over an hour and he came out and gave me the permit. I was surprised at the speed in which my permit was granted because I knew that the process took up to two months and that applicants were required to produce two shop guarantees.

I left Shanghai on December 9, 1949, and arrived in Hong Kong on December 23 after a rough 1,300-

mile overland trip by train and bus via Nanchang, Kian, Kanchow, Kukong and Canton. The trip took me through three provinces and closely followed the route of the communist thrust through Kiangsi into Kwangtung.

In Kanchow, Kiangsi province, where the communists apparently are maintaining a large garrison against the bandits and guerrillas roving the countryside, I was irritated by a communist regulation requiring all rickshaw passengers to disembark at the city gate, walk through the gate and board the rickshaw again at the other side. I pointed out to the guards that that was what the Japanese used to do to the Chinese people during the old occupation days. He smiled and said, "It is an order from our superiors".

Nightly curfew from eleven to five was imposed in all the towns I passed through. In Nanchang, the curfew was announced by air raid sirens.

I found the same kind of post-liberation conditions in all the towns I passed through as I had found in the Nanking-Shanghai area: business depression, unemployment, heavy taxes, levies and widespread disillusionment and discontent with communist rule.

In Nanchang and Canton, the communists made a new levy on the populace, which they had not introduced in Nanking and Shanghai – cash loans. The city of Nanchang was required to give two cash loans to the communists amounting to RMB$24 billion (US$6 million) at the prevailing exchange rate. In Canton, the cash loans were said to be much larger.

In Nanchang, communist rule is not as lenient and liberal as in Shanghai. There the shop assistants and apprentices have already been regimented into the "learning movement". The communists also frequently conducted "investigations of thought" among intelligentsia. One member of the intelligentsia said that two favourite questions of communist investigators were whether Soviet Russia is imperialistic and whether a third world war would break out. He said most of the intelligentsia, who knew in advance of the communist attitude on these questions, answered no to both questions.

The communists have established a "university" in Nanchang called the Eight-One (August 1st) University. It is named after the day in 1927 when the communist army was formed in the city. The communists once held a discussion in the "university" on whether a third world war would break out and, if it broke out, whether Soviet Russia would win. Communists posted posters all over the meeting hall encouraging participants to express their opinions with candour and courage. Many participants did. Some of them maintained that a third world war would break out and that the Soviets would lose. These people were the next day tried as "Kuomintang special service agents".

The communists in Nanchang had renamed the Nationalist Chungcheng University (named after Generalissimo Chiang Kai-shek) Nanchang University. All former professors were retained at their posts, except for political science professors, who were put into an indoctrination camp for three months and then discharged.

One resident told me that people in the city have stored away their Western suits and are putting on only coarse cloth Chinese gowns, because when a man puts on a Western suit the communists suspect him of having connections with the United States.

The communists appear to have been able to control the population and order has been restored almost to normal in Kiangsi. There are a few guerrilla units operating in the hilly regions in the southern part of the province, but not enough to threaten highway or rail communications.

In Kwangtung, however, the communists do not seem to have brought the province under effective control. Highway robbery, banditry and some scattered anti-communist irregulars still populate the countryside. The provincial capital, Canton, is also in disorder, although conditions have improved lately. Robbers and pickpockets operate on the streets even in daylight. Just two days before I arrived in Canton, an armed band robbed a warehouse inside the city of nineteen drums of gasoline at eight-thirty in the morning.

There were practically no police in the Canton streets. During my three-day stay there from December 21 to 23, 1949, I saw only three unarmed traffic policemen. A local Chinese said that the police are now in an indoctrination camp. There are also very few Liberation Army men guarding the streets. I was warned by the hotel boy not to go into the streets after dark. Most shops open at eleven in the morning and close by five in the afternoon.

Several Chinese in Canton told me that some of the outlaws now disrupting public order in the city are former communist guerrillas who are dissatisfied because they were asked to disband and hand in their arms. They said that the old professional robbers and pickpockets are also intensifying their lawlessness as a result of the communist policy of sponsoring the poor.

In southern parts of Kiangsi, the endless string of blockhouses built by Chiang Kai-shek in the early 1930s in his suppression campaigns against the communists are still there, though in a dilapidated state. In Kwangtung, I saw a blockhouse in practically every village, built by the villagers as a self-defence measure against banditry. Every village maintains an armed guard and the communists expect to have a difficult time making the people surrender their private arms to the state.

Another problem for the communists in Kwangtung, especially in Canton, is how to make the people accept the *renminbi* currency. Hong Kong currency notes are still in circulation despite the official ban. The communists have opened a propaganda campaign with the help of students and workers against the Hong Kong dollar.

My first experience with the effects of communist rule in Nanchang was the rickshaw racketeering there, which had become worse since the communists took over the city. I and other newcomers to the town were charged ten times the normal fare. When I arrived at the railway station, I tried to fight off the rickshaw racketeering by asking my hotel to hire a truck to carry my luggage from the station. The hotel man refused to do it because, he explained, trucks had been to the railway station before and manhandled by the rickshaw men. He said the rickshaw pullers regarded the trucks as capitalists out to exploit them.

Once, a rickshaw puller asked me, upon arrival at my hotel, for a much higher fare than had been originally agreed upon. When I refused to pay he resorted to bullying methods. I was about to bring my grievance to the police when a hotel boy stopped me. He said, "Don't go to the police. They always side with the labouring class".

The communists seemed to have done a good job in restoring rail communications, though many sections and bridges were repaired in a makeshift manner and the train sometimes has to go at a dead slow pace. Many bridges across the Chi and Kan rivers in Kiangsi were washed away by the recent floods and our bus had to cross the rivers on ferries. When we arrived at the Kan River, there were about forty commercial trucks queued up at the ferry. Some trucks had waited for five days. Priority to use the ferry is given to army vehicles. When our bus, which belonged to the government-operated transportation bureau, arrived the ferry man gave us permission to cross ahead of the commercial trucks. But the communist soldiers guarding the ferry refused to approve the permission. Fortunately, we had two Liberation Army men as passengers. They went down to talk to their comrades and we were allowed to cross immediately.

I regret that I had not paid a visit to Peking during my eight months' stay in communist China. Many friends had advised me to go there to see how things are changing under the new regime, but I decided not to act on their advice. The ban against the foreign press is still in force there and one cannot predict what the communists would do even if one were there for a personal visit.

My wife, however, visited Peking for a week before we left. From what she observed the city seems to be now under very tight police rule. As in Soviet Russia, the police carry out checks on the people around two or three in the morning. If someone has a guest at his house for more than three nights, he must report it to the police. One man was made to "wait" in the police station overnight for failing to do so. One of our friends, an extremely sociable girl, aroused the suspicion of the police because too many people came to her house. She was checked twice at three o'clock in the morning.

All of the civil servants and factory workers in Peking are working ten hours or more a day on meagre pay. They must get up at five-thirty a.m., rush through their toilet and breakfast and go to the office where they must stay until seven in the evening. Sometimes there is a special meeting and they must stay well into the night.

One of our friends is working in the police station. She works twelve hours a day, six days a week. Frequently she works on Sundays, too. She is allowed to go home only once a week, and her salary is the cash equivalent of 150 catties of millet, which is equivalent to approximately US$10. Most of our friends in Peking are showing signs of over-work and under-nourishment. My wife's observation is that if they continue this kind of life, they will end up TB cases.

In addition to keeping a close check on the people living in the city, the communist police are especially suspicious of visitors. Visitors must report to the police immediately upon arrival, state the purpose of their visit and obtain authorisation to stay for a certain length of time. When the time expires, a visitor may request an extension, but obtaining one is extremely difficult. Unless a man has a job in the city, it is no longer possible for him to remain in Peking.

One of our friends, who was a member of the Municipal Council under the Kuomintang, is undergoing a process of "thought reform" under close communist police surveillance. She has been required to study communist books and write periodical articles for the perusal of the police to see how far her "reactionary thought" has been reformed. The police visit her periodically and always about three o'clock in the morning to check whether she is at home and to question her on the progress of her "thought reform". She is not allowed outside the city gates. This close police surveillance is beginning to get on her nerves and she is worn down physically as well. From what we know of her, she is not politically-minded, despite her membership in the Kuomintang Municipal Council. She was elected to the Council, not because she wanted the job but because friends wanted her to take the job, and now she is suffering the consequences of taking her friends' advice.

Peking is now a city of bicycles. Most people sell what they can spare or use their savings to buy bicycles, because cycling to the office is cheaper than taking the buses or pedicabs. Very few people can afford to ride pedicabs and, as a consequence, pedicab fares are one of the cheapest commodities in Peking.

The communists have created a new atmosphere in Peking. They have repainted the historic palaces and cleaned the public parks. Workers parade the streets frequently, and school children fill the town with communist songs.

Under the new atmosphere, however, there is a strong current of dissatisfaction with the communists. Shopkeepers talk openly of how conditions have deteriorated since the Japanese occupation. Discontent among workers has found open expression in the many sabotage activities inside and outside the city; for example, the wreckage of the Shihchingshan coal mine generators and the destruction of scores of buses of the city transportation bureau. My wife called on a professor of the National Tsinghua University to ask him how things are going. He said, "Much the same as before, except that we have to be very cautious in what we say and do in private conversations and in classes".

Communist Chairman Mao Tse-tung has his "Kremlin" in the Western Hills in the suburbs of the city, where other top communist leaders also live. The Western Hills is a famous scenic spot and a popular summer resort with a great number of modern bungalows, built by foreigners and rich Chinese officials. This scenic spot is now closed to the public.